# ETHEREUM 2.0 INVESTING

## BY NFT TRENDING CRYPTO ART

"An investment in knowledge pays the best interest"

- Benjamin Franklin.

# GET A FREE AUDIOBOOK

EMAIL SUBJECT LINE:

"ETH 2.0"

TO

MINDSETMASTERSHIP@GMAIL.COM

# JOIN OUR

## NFT, CRYPTO ART,

## METAVERSE & DEFI

## Entrepreneur Power Group

To help reinforce the learning's from our books, I strongly suggest you join our well-informed powerhouse community on Facebook.

Here, you will connect and share with other like-minded people to support your journey and help you grow.

>>>CLICK BELOW to join Our NFT Group <<<

### News Site & Community Group:

https://www.facebook.com/groups/nfttrending/

Want Future Book Releases?

Email us at:

mindsetmastership@gmail.com

Find us on Instagram!

@MindsetMastership

MASTERSHIP BOOKS

UK | USA | Canada | Ireland | Australia

India | New Zealand | South Africa | China

Mastership Books is part of the United Arts Publishing House group of companies based in London, England, UK.

First published by Mastership Books (London, UK), 2022

I S B N: 978-1-915002-30-3

Cover design by Rich © United Arts Publishing (UK)

Text and internal design by Rich © United Arts Publishing (UK)

Image credits reserved.

Colour separation by Spitting Image Design Studio

Printed and bound in Great Britain

National Publications Association of Britain

London, England, United Kingdom.

Paper design UAP
ISBN: 978-1-915002-30-3
(paperback)
A723.5

Title: Ethereum 2.0 Investing
Design, Bound & Printed:
London, England,
Great Britain.

"If you really want to invest in something today, start investing your knowledge in **NFTs**, **Metaverse, Blockchain, Crypto** and **DeFi**, these hidden treasure's are going mainstream"

# Contents

# INTRODUCTION

**Meaning of Ethereum 2.0**

Ethereum 2.0, also called Serenity or ETH 2.0, is a multi-level update to Ethereum. Its main goal is to increase Ethereum's transaction capacity, lower fees, and make the network more sustainable. To achieve this, Ethereum will switch from proof-of-work (PoW) to proof-of-stake consensus (PoS).

**Consensus Mechanism**

Databases are commonly used by businesses and organizations to store user information such as emails, names, and addresses. Database servers are usually housed in a single location and are managed by a single person or a small group of administrators. A blockchain is a kind of database, but instead of having all its information in one central location under the supervision and control of a few people, it is distributed across many people and places. If one computer fails, there are plenty of others to keep the data and network running.

These people must figure out how to agree on the correct set of data so that their versions of it all match. Some procedure is required to reach this agreement. Blockchains use a variety of consensus procedures to guarantee that data (in the instance of a cryptocurrency, this data is transactions) is consistent across all nodes (individual computers) in the system.

## Ethereum Technological Revolution

The switch to Proof-of-Stake as a consensus mechanism was one of the most significant changes brought about by the introduction of ETH2. We must first look at Ethereum's first consensus process to know why this is significant.

## Brief About Proof-of-Work

Since its development, proof-of-Work (PoW) has been Ethereum's default consensus mechanism. In other words, PoW is a protocol that aids in reaching network consensus. PoW uses so-called miners to do this. Miners are the owners of powerful computers connected to the blockchain network, and they compete against one another to solve complicated mathematical puzzles and are paid for their efforts. Simply put, PoW validates transactions by using computational power.

However, there are two significant disadvantages of PoW:

## Energy Usage

PoW needs lots of energy when thousands of powerful computers are engaged in the process, which is detrimental to the environment. In 2018, when it was traded the most, Ethereum consumed more than 20 TW/h. In 2017, the whole country of Ireland consumed 26 TWh of energy yearly. The good news is that this has improved over time with Ethereum, but Bitcoin's PoW consensus has been consuming 70+ TWh at peak traffic periods for the past two years. When you convert that to comparable emissions, BTC and ETH become significant pollutants.

## Security Issues

While Bitcoin and Ethereum are extensive networks where 51 percent assaults are nearly impossible, other tiny networks might be targeted, giving the attacker enough mining power to change the rules. Fortunately, PoW wasn't the only consensus method available, so the Ethereum network's developers chose Proof-of-Stake as a more secure and environmentally friendly option.

## The Coming of Proof-of-Stake

With an expanding number of users and many transactions, Ethereum required a more efficient consensus mechanism, and Proof-of-Stake appeared to be the ideal solution. Serenity's principal purpose was to switch from PoW to PoS. Interestingly, we don't need miners for PoS, and there's no need to use any of your computer's resources. The simplest explanation for PoS is that economic incentives are critical to the model's success. Users who wish to help run the network will stake ETH and be assigned the validator function.

The validator will validate transactions just like in PoW systems. They will be rewarded for their work in gas fees and block rewards, similar to how "miners" were compensated in the previous version of Ethereum with ETH. The Beacon Chain brought the PoS consensus to the Ethereum network, and you can think of it as a foundation for future network enhancements. In other words, it will aid in the expansion of ETH2 and the development of shard chains and other technologies.

## The Current State of Ethereum 2.0

Three upgrades have been added to the Beacon Chain since its debut on December 1, 2020: The Berlin upgrade, the London upgrade, and the Altair upgrade.

### Berlin Upgrade

The Berlin update went live on April 15, 2021, and it reduced the cost of gas for various EVM (Ethereum Virtual Machine) operations. It improves several transaction types as part of the update.

### London Upgrade

The London update went live on August 5, 2021, and it included EIP-1559, which reformed the transaction fee market for the ETH 1.0 chain. Gas fees for specified services were also eliminated or lowered.

### Altair Upgrade

Altair, the most recent update, was released on October 27, 2021. The Altair update is Ethereum's Beacon Chain's first planned upgrade. It includes support for "sync committees," enabling light clients, bringing validator inactivity up to maximum levels, and reducing penalties.

### Burned Ethereum and the Consensus Layer

In addition to the London Hard Fork, Ethereum is nearing its most complete form. Ethereum 2.0, which was recently renamed Consensus Layer, will speed up transactions, reduce prices, and end Ethereum's carbon or energy footprint problem. The upgrade will switch Ethereum from a proof-of-work (PoW) consensus process to a proof-of-stake model. The latter mechanism is less harmful to the environment since it requires less computational resources to provide equivalent levels of security.

Another exciting aspect of switching to proof-of-stake is that proof-of-work requires many Ethers to incentivize people with large infrastructure to lend their resources and validate transactions on the network. If you have a light infrastructure, you can issue a lot less Ether for each block on the network. With less supply, fewer Ethereum coins will be available on the market. This, along with the current burn process, means that Ethereum will burn more Ether every day than is issued. It will provide much less Ether to protect the network. As a result, ultra-sound money is going to be created. According to the Ethereum co-founder, these upgrades will be implemented by Q2 or maybe Q3 of 2022.

### ETH2 Validator

Everyone who wishes to be a part of Ethereum 2.0's consensus system will need to deposit 32 ETH into their Ethereum Foundation, the official Ethereum 2.0 deposit contract. However, depending on the current value of ETH, 32 ETH might be a significant sum of money. As a result, you may stake even less if you wish, but you'll need to employ a staking pool to combine your resources with other stakeholders to influence the network significantly. Staking as little as 0.01 ETH is possible in some of these pools.

Staking services exist that can assist you in becoming a validator by placing your ETH in a staking pool. You're probably thinking about how much money you'll make as a validator right now. The amount of ETH mainly determines the response invested in the system. If less than a million ETH is committed, the yearly payouts might be above 18 percent. As people invest more ETH in the system, this will decrease. The annual incentive will be 1.81 percent or even less until more than 100 million ETH are in the system.

## Benefits of Proof of Stake

Proof-of-Stake was a significant shift in the Ethereum network, and its authors feel it was always going to happen since it addressed three fundamental issues with Ethereum 1.0. Let's have a look at how PoS helped to improve the network.

## Better Sustainability

PoS doesn't need miners to solve complex arithmetic problems with thousands-of-dollar programming resources, damaging the environment. No other energy-intensive processes are necessary to participate in the network.

## Increased Security

With a PoS consensus mechanism, 51 % of attacks are considerably more difficult, as attackers will require a lot of money to carry them out. It's still theoretically conceivable, but it's highly improbable.

## Scalability

Proof of stake makes sharding possible, which would be impossible to achieve if Ethereum stuck with the Proof of work approach. You're presumably not familiar with sharding. For clarity, sharding is the Ethereum network's second-largest improvement after PoS, so it deserves its section.

## Sharding - A Solution to Scalability

Sharding will aid the network's ability to execute transactions and store data in ETH2. When there is a lot of traffic, PoW blockchains like Bitcoin and ETH1.0 are prone to congestion, and transactions become slower as the network struggles to keep up with the growing number of users. Sharding is the answer to this problem. Vitalik Buterin (the cofounder of Ethereum) has already guaranteed significantly faster transaction times, although it is yet to be deployed. Here's the comparison:

15 TPS on Ethereum 1.0 (transactions per second)

100,000 TPS on Ethereum 2.0

Before we go into the details, let us look at the scalability problem PoW model-based networks have.

## Proof-of-Work Scalability Issues and Possible Solutions

Proof-of-Work was a flawless consensus mechanism when Bitcoin was developed. Because there were few Bitcoin transactions initially, everything went well. When the number of transactions began to rise, the first problem arose. This happened for the first time in 2017 for both BTC and ETH when the bull run pushed both cryptocurrencies to their all-time highs. This resulted in slower transactions and higher gas fees on the ETH network. When DeFi as a concept became famous in 2020, the same thing happened.

Both times, the discussion of scalability was unavoidable since the network failed to deliver the best possible service due to the high volume of transactions. The two possible solutions for staying on PoW and increasing scalability are:

- Increasing block size
- Off-chain scaling

**Increase Block Size**

Initially, blocks were only 1 MB in size; however, this was subsequently raised to satisfy demand. Increasing the block size is one of the options. However, this is only a temporary solution since you have to increase the block size as the number of transactions grows. This would necessitate more network capacity and greater centralization, providing those with faster connections an advantage.

**Off-chain Scaling**

You can build new payment channels that aren't connected to the blockchain when the volume of transactions gets too large for on-chain processing. While this appears to be a logical approach, it questions the blockchain's existence. The only viable long-term option was to implement Proof-of-Stake and devise a procedure to allow transactions to be completed considerably more quickly.

**Evolution of Ethereum**

At the age of 19, Vitalik Buterin came up with the concept of Ethereum. Later that year, he released a white paper defining Ethereum as a next-generation smart contract and decentralized application platform, officially launching Ethereum. Ethereum is currently the second-largest cryptocurrency in market value, accounting for around 18% of the market. Its success is due to a brilliantly elegant idea, a well-executed development process, and the community's continuing support.

Let's look back at Ethereum's evolution and provide predictions for the future of Ethereum 2.0.

**Pre-launch**

Unarguably, Bitcoin was the inspiration for Ethereum's creation. Bitcoin laid the groundwork for blockchain technology that is decentralized. However, its capabilities are restricted to peer-to-peer electronic currency transactions. Buterin intended to extend blockchain's capability to programmable ideas after noticing this constraint.

Initially, he planned to do this by layering a more powerful programming language on top of Bitcoin to handle smart contracts, but the Bitcoin community rejected this concept. Buterin then planned to develop a brand-new blockchain to power this "global computer." Buterin presented his white paper explaining the Ethereum concept in late 2013. He then launched Ethereum originally in January 2014 during the North American Bitcoin Conference in Miami. It attracted the interest of many developers, notably Gavin Wood, who released the renowned "Yellow Paper" on Ethereum's technical implementation.

By the end of 2014, Ethereum had completed its first crowdfunding campaign, raising more than $18 million through the sale of its native coin, Ether. The inaugural Ethereum conference, named DEVCON0, was also held by early Ethereum founders and developers, during which the developers first met.

## Execution

Ethereum's evolution may be divided into four stages. Each step denotes a network-wide update necessary at some point, after which outdated versions will no longer be supported. Another name for them is "hard forks." Within the significant stages, there have been both planned and unplanned sub-upgrades.

## Frontier Phase

On July 30, 2015, the first version of Ethereum (Ethereum 1.0), called Frontier, was released. Its two main functions enabled users to mine Ether and execute smart contracts. The first stage aimed to get the network up and operating so that miners could begin mining and developers could test their decentralized apps (DApps). Frontier Thawing was a minor fork that limited gas to 5,000 per transaction to keep transaction costs from becoming prohibitively expensive and limiting utilization.

## Homestead Phase

If Frontier was the "safer" version of Frontier, Homestead was the "functioning" version of Ethereum. This phase brought Ethereum's security flaw to the public's notice with the DAO breach. DAO was an innovative idea that was launched in 2016 to allow users to crowdsource monies. It failed, however, owing to a flaw in its smart contract code, which hackers used to steal a portion of the organization's cash. As a result of this event, a contentious decision was made to initiate a hard fork on the Ethereum network to retrieve the stolen money. Some community members protested the move, which resulted in the establishment of the Ethereum Classic, which is still in use today.

Tangerine Whistle and Spurious Dragon were launched following a series of DoS (denial-of-service) attacks to address security issues by adjusting gas costs and adding state clearing.

**Metropolis Phase**

The Ethereum security, privacy, and scalability were all improved with Metropolis, and it addressed many of Ethereum's scalability issues and provided developers and consumers with a lighter, more efficient experience. Due to its complexity, they issued the upgrade in two stages: Byzantium and Constantinople. Byzantium was the initial stage, with nine patches including major changes, also known as Ethereum improvement protocols (EIP). Important innovations like zk-SNARKs, account abstraction, and the difficulty bomb were among them.

Constantinople was planned to be released in mid-2018, but it was delayed for more than a year due to a severe issue discovered only hours before it was released. Constantinople was established to address any issues that could develop due to Byzantium's implementation. It also established the framework for Ethereum's move from PoW to PoS, dramatically lowering the amount of energy required for Ethereum's validation.

**Serenity Phase**

The Serenity stage is currently under construction. This version, also known as Ethereum 2.0, attempts to get Ethereum to a point where you can use it without causing security or high-volume difficulties. It tries to solve two significant problems that Ethereum is currently facing: a crowded network that can only handle a limited number of transactions per second (with higher gas fees for faster transactions) and reduce the excessive energy consumption associated with the PoW mechanism.

The switch from PoW to PoS and the creation of shard chains, which will share the network's workload, are two key advancements. Ethereum 2.0 intends to be more scalable, safe, and long-term, yet when (or if) it will launch and other difficulties are unknown.

## Differences Between Ethereum 1.0 And 2.0

The responses to the question "What is Ethereum 2.0?" do not address the technical elements of how it differs from Ethereum 1.0. Two significant enhancements have been made in ETH 2.0, ensuring the intended outcomes and proof of Stake consensus and sharding are two of the essential improvements.

Here's a quick rundown of the two major enhancements in ETH 2.0.

## Proof of Stake Consensus

As briefly discussed previously, instead of the Proof of Work consensus used in Ethereum 1.0, Ethereum 2.0 employs the Proof of Stake consensus. Proof of Work consensus necessitates using physical computer power from miners and electricity to develop blockchain blocks. On the other hand, PoS does not rely on miners or power. In the section on how ETH 2.0 works, you'll learn more about Proof of Stake.

**Shard Chains**

Sharding is another significant feature in ETH 2.0. In reality, shard chains are one of the main drivers of Ethereum's scalability advances. The current construction of single chains with consecutive blocks provides greater security and makes information verification easier. On the other side, requiring each transaction to traverse through every complete node on a blockchain in successive blocks might slow down transactions. Since they're responsible for many scalability improvements, shard chains are a big deal in Ethereum 2.0 news.

Sharding is a way of partitioning the Ethereum blockchain to distribute data processing responsibilities evenly across multiple nodes. Instead of processing transactions sequentially, shard chains allow them to be processed parallel. Ethereum 2.0's capability for better parallel processing might result in increased throughput.

**Roadmap for Ethereum 2.0**

Given its compelling value benefits, it's understandable to be concerned about ETH 2.0's launch. Is Ethereum 2.0 on the way? Wasn't it supposed to be out in December 2020? You aren't the only one who has these questions. If you examine it critically, you will notice that ETH 2.0 is not a new blockchain network superior to Ethereum 1.0. Ethereum 2.0, on the other hand, is a series of enhancements that are being handed out in stages. To grasp the significance of ETH 2.0, you'll need a clear picture of its trajectory. Let's look at the various stages of the ETH 2.0 roadmap to see when it will be fully operational.

## Beacons Chain

The first phase drew much attention in Ethereum 2.0 news, mainly because of the ETH 2.0 hype. Ethereum implemented the new Beacon Chain, or Proof of Stake consensus layer, during this phase. On the Beacon Chain, each validator represents a 32 ETH stake, and the Beacon Chain currently has 222,052 validators. Surprisingly, the Proof of Work chain can coexist with the new PoS chain without compromising data consistency.

## Merging Beacon Chain with Mainnet

It is expected that The Beacon Chain will merge with the Ethereum Mainnet in the next step of the Ethereum 2.0 roadmap. With intentions to release Ethereum 2.0 in the first half of 2022, the merger gives a credible response to the question, "Is Ethereum 2.0 coming out?" Transactions and applications will resume as usual following the integration.

## Shard Chains

The scalability phase would be the ultimate stage in the growth of Ethereum 2.0. While the Beacon Chain and Merge can help with sustainability and continuity, shard chains will address the issue of scalability. Currently, the plan for ETH 2.0 implies that the scaling phase might begin in late 2022. Shard chains will allow long-term increases in data storage and access capacity. In addition, the ETH 2.0 scalability plan emphasizes layer 2 solutions like rollups.

## Myths About the Merge

Here are three typical misunderstandings that have been debunked.

- The merger will create no new Ethereum token

One common misperception is that Ethereum would have a "new" coin after the merger. Ether (ETH), Ethereum's cryptocurrency, will stay unchanged. The Ethereum Foundation published instructions regarding how the merging should be described because of this misunderstanding around a "new" coin. The merger was previously known as "Ethereum 2.0" or "Eth2." However, the Ethereum Foundation and the blockchain's core developers declared that this labelling would be phased away. Many fraudsters attempted to persuade consumers that a new "Eth2" token would be separate from ETH, which was incorrect.

In a blog post, the Ethereum Foundation stated, "Unfortunately, bad actors have sought to utilize the Eth2 misnomer to defraud consumers by informing them to trade their ETH for 'ETH2' tokens or that they must somehow relocate their ETH before the Eth2 upgrade."

Investors should be wary of outsiders' promises about an airdrop or free tokens relating to the merger.

- The merger will not result in a reduction in Ethereum's fees

Another myth is that the merger will decrease "gas costs," or transaction fees, for Ethereum. This is also incorrect. The merge will merely change Ethereum's proof-of-stake mechanism from proof-of-work to proof-of-stake. Ethereum presently uses proof-of-work, which requires miners to solve complicated problems to validate transactions and issue new currency. This mechanism necessitates a significant amount of computer processing power which has a negative environmental effect.

Ethereum will upgrade to proof-of-stake, which will allow users to confirm transactions based on how many coins they contribute or stake. Users who stake more coins have a better chance of being selected to validate transactions on the network and earning a reward. According to David Lawant, director of research at Bitwise Asset Management, "The Merge is Ethereum's most major improvement." "Every crypto network must decide how it will select, in a decentralized manner, who will submit a new block of transactions for all members to confirm and add to the blockchain." The Merge will signal the transition of Ethereum from proof-of-work to proof-of-stake."

Ethereum presently has two chains running in parallel: PoW and PoS. While both chains include validators, the proof-of-work chain is presently the only one that handles user transactions. After integrating, Ethereum's blockchain will entirely transition to the proof-of-stake Beacon Chain, rendering mining useless. Many people may anticipate that this change in structure would lower the cost of "gas fees," which may add hundreds of dollars to the cost of executing Ether transactions depending on how crowded the network is.

- There is no predetermined date for the merger to take place

Despite much conjecture, there is currently no official schedule for the merge. Some speculate that it will happen this June, but you should only trust the Ethereum Foundation's word on established dates. "It is conceivable that frauds [and] bogus announcements will come up in the following months.

The unclear timescale is due to the amount of planning necessary for the merger. After all, the merger's success is critical since Ethereum is responsible for many things, including a considerable amount of money. It not only enables popular decentralized finance (DeFi) apps and non-fungible tokens but also powers Ether, the second-largest cryptocurrency (NFTs). Ethereum developers have conducted several tests and updates to guarantee that the merging goes successfully. This is a major engineering project, and such projects need a great deal of testing and planning. 'It will happen when it's ready' is frequently the slogan for such project regular updates.

**Advantages of Ethereum 2.0**

Ethereum 2.0 will provide a slew of new features that will likely entice even more developers to join the network. The following are the three significant enhancements:

**Greater Scalability**

Ethereum must be able to handle thousands of transactions per second (TPS) for applications to run faster and with lower costs. Due to the inclusion of more nodes, the one-two punch of sharding and a PoS algorithm is predicted to provide more scalability, resulting in higher TPS without requiring more power.

**Better Security**

To combat assaults, Ethereum must be as safe as possible so that users, especially institutions, feel comfortable using it. The Beacon Chain, as previously indicated, is intended to aid network security.

## Greater Sustainability

A smaller carbon footprint has become a prominent issue in the bitcoin sector. The PoW consensus algorithm is relatively energy-intensive. Because there will be no more mining in Ethereum 2.0, it will benefit the environment. Ethereum's energy usage will be reduced "by a factor of more than 1,000" using PoS, according to Ethereum Co-Founder Vitalik Buterin.

## Ethereum 2.0 to Attract Institutions

We expect the mainnet launch to occur by the end of June, following the successful completion of the merging test run. Observers predict that institutional adoption will rise after the Eth 2.0 upgrade is completed. Estimates for post-merger yield range from 10% to 20%. Furthermore, institutions will find it simpler to embrace proof-of-stake since they will no longer have to explain the energy consumption element of the investment argument connected with bitcoin and proof-of-work currencies.

PoS is a more ecologically friendly consensus process than PoW, which compensates miners with tokens for solving challenging mathematical problems to confirm transactions. That procedure needs a lot of energy. According to some studies, bitcoin mining has a carbon footprint comparable to affluent countries, deterring institutions from adopting the money. Last year, Tesla, a leading electric vehicle manufacturer in the United States, halted bitcoin payments due to environmental worries about mining.

Staking was introduced via the Beacon Chain (deposit contract published in December 2020), but it does not affect how Ethereum functions fundamentally. That all changes in 2022, when it joins with the mainnet, resulting in a considerable consensus change, a 99.95 percent reduction in energy usage, and the elimination of a carbon footprint the size of Finland.

## Implications for Crypto Investors

Ethereum's next update may make it more appealing to institutional investors and increase public interest in the cryptocurrency sector. The improved network will be able to use sharding, a method of lowering transaction fees, which has been a critical hurdle to the widespread adoption of the Ethereum network. Because it will use the more environmentally friendly proof of stake technique for confirming transactions, Ethereum 2.0 may become more appealing to institutional investors. The transition to proof of stake will let institutional investors invest in Ethereum since it will meet environmental, social, and corporate governance (ESG) requirements.

The world's second-largest cryptocurrency by market capitalization is now confirming transactions on its blockchain using the energy-intensive proof of work process. For the world's leading financial institutions subject to ESG promises, the energy-intensive proof of work system has been a barrier to entry. This merger will be the most significant software change in the eight-year history of Ethereum (ETH-USD). Switching to proof of stake will reduce the amount of energy used by the Ethereum network by 99.9%.

Because there will be no more mining rewards due to the proof of work consensus process, there will be fewer ether tokens created every year due to the switch to proof of stake. It will reduce the issuance of new ether tokens by 90% under Ethereum 2.0, and the annual issuance will shrink from around 5 million to 0.5 million ethers. This will cause Ethereum to become deflationary, which is fantastic news for cryptocurrency investors because every investor wants an appreciating asset.

**Ethereum Token Price Prediction**

Ethereum is the most well-known altcoin, and it represents much more to many investors and enthusiasts than just another cryptocurrency. Experts believe that by 2022, its value will have soared by 400%. Since its debut, the value of Ether (ETH), Ethereum's native asset, has surged. Ether, a cryptocurrency founded by computer engineer Vitalik Buterin, has surged in value from $0.311 at its debut in 2015 to over $4,800 at its most recent peak late last year, despite significant volatility.

According to the crypto news site Coinpedia, if the same bullish run that began in mid-2021 continues, ETH might end 2022 between $6,500 and $7,500. However, the crypto sector had a negative drop in 2022, indicating that Ethereum's price would not arise solely due to good feelings. While the Ethereum team works to transition to a second-generation version, the blockchain now confronts intense competition from analogous platforms that fill in the gaps.

If Ethereum's imminent transition to Ethereum 2.0 is successful, Coinpedia estimates a price of $12,962.33 in 2022. The additional features might make Ethereum more economical for consumers to mint and build goods, as Ethereum's transaction fees are infamously high presently.

**Key Takeaways**

- Ethereum 2.0 marks the transition to a new consensus model called "proof-of-stake."

- Compared to the earlier proof-of-work paradigm, proof-of-stake enables quicker transactions and reduced costs.

- The proof-of-stake approach allows Ethereum investors to "stake" their assets into "stake pools" to collect rewards and expand their holdings over time.

- Several prominent exchanges, including Kraken, Coinbase, and Binance, are currently accepting Ethereum stakes.

- Ethereum 2.0 will use a mechanism known as sharding to substantially accelerate transaction speeds, perhaps reaching 100,000 transactions per second or more.

- The present cost of transactions on the Ethereum network is prohibitive for many. If this update is effective, the lower prices will make the network more accessible to regular users.

- Because of the cheaper costs and speedier transactions, Ethereum's update might significantly impact its price.

# CHAPTER 1

## ETHEREUM ARCHITECTURE

**Proof of Stake Vs Proof of Work**

Proof-of-work was the initial approach used by Bitcoin for blockchain consensus. Miners, who give their computer processing power, such as graphics processing units (GPUs) and central processing units (CPUs), perform complex algorithms and validate blocks in the PoW system. Within a blockchain network, blocks retain a specific number of transactions, and miners validate and log blocks on the blockchain when they are full. Each block of transactions must be certified unique to avoid double-spending or duplicate transactions. Each block has a 64-digit hexadecimal code that proves its uniqueness, but miners must locate it. The proof-of-work moniker refers to the employment of miner machines' computing capacity to crack the hexadecimal code. A computer uses actual power to do calculations and solve problems.

However, mining for blocks is not particularly ecologically friendly, and it consumes a lot of energy and dramatically boosts a miner's electricity expenses. Mining cryptocurrency is also a competition, and miners using a single graphics card are up against organizations with hundreds, if not thousands, of graphics cards. Only the first miner to uncover the code receives a reward in Bitcoin, making it difficult for anyone without a lot of money to invest in a competent mining setup.

Proof-of-stake resolves many of the problems associated with the PoW consensus approach. In Proof-of-Stake, which is similar to mining, users must validate transactions. Validators, on the other hand, are PoS network participants. Validators are users who stake, or lock in, a particular amount of bitcoin into the network. These users notify the network that they want to be validators to lock in money. The more cash pledged by a validator, the more incentives these users receive for their participation. Users that engage in a network as validators are responsible for validating network transactions. Once a validator authorizes a transaction, it is sent to the blockchain, and the validator is rewarded. PoS is more accessible than PoW because it does not require expensive hardware, and anyone who has the funds can participate.

As more users connect to the network and validate transactions, network accessibility improves scalability. A network with more people validating it is more secure and decentralized. A PoS network has an expanding number of stable sites rather than a single central point for bad actors to attack. A PoS network is also better for the environment than a PoW network because it uses less electricity. More network decentralization also protects against what is known as a 51 percent attack, which occurs when a bad actor acquires control of 51 percent of nodes on a PoW network and confirms malicious transactions. In some aspects, proof-of-stake avoids a 51 percent attack because it requires holding 51 percent of the network's tokens. Having 51 percent of all tokens on a PoS network sounds nearly unfeasible, as it would need stealing from hundreds of Ethereum wallets all at once.

After the update, Ethereum will have access to all proof-of-stake features. PoS will improve Ethereum's scalability, accessibility, and security while reducing its environmental impact. However, converting Ethereum to a 2.0 network is no simple undertaking, needing a great deal of user input and a significant amount of time for changes to take effect.

## Transitioning to Ethereum 2.0

You can divide the move to Ethereum 2.0 into many parts.

## Phase 0

The Beacon Chain is introduced in Ethereum 2.0's Phase 0 upgrade. The Beacon Chain, which went live on December 1, 2020, represents the PoS transition by allowing users to stake (lock away) their Ethereum and become validators. The Beacon Chain coexists with Ethereum's mainnet; Phase 0 does not affect the main Ethereum blockchain. However, the Beacon chain and mainnet will eventually be united. The idea is to "merge" Mainnet and the Beacon Chain's coordinated proof-of-stake technique.

Additionally, potential validators can still stake 32 ETH to express their interest in the Beacon Chain. It's a big ask to ask clients to invest 32 ETH, tens of thousands of dollars in Ethereum. The system will keep staked money for at least two years before releasing it when Ethereum 2.0 is fully operational. We anticipate that the strict entry standards will attract early validators enthusiastic about the project's future.

## Phase 1

The first phase was planned to begin in mid-2021, but developers moved it back to early 2022, citing incomplete work and code auditing as major reasons for the delay. In this stage, the Beacon Chain will be joined with the mainnet, formally moving to a PoS consensus process. Starting with Phase 1, Eth2 will store Ethereum's whole transaction history and allow smart contracts on the PoS network. As mining is removed from the Ethereum 2.0 network, stakers and validators will formally take over. We anticipate that many miners will stake their shares to become validators. The addition of sharding was planned for Phase 1 of the Ethereum 2.0 upgrade. Sharding is dividing a colossal database, such as the blockchain, into smaller chains called shards. Eth2 will have 64 shards, which implies the system's load will be distributed across 64 different chains. Shards make running a node easier by lowering the hardware requirements. This upgrade will occur after the mainnet, and the Beacon Chain have merged.

Validators and other users can operate their shards on Ethereum 2.0, validating transactions and preventing congestion on the mainchain. A proof-of-stake consensus technique is necessary for shard networks to enter the Ethereum ecosystem safely. Staking will be implemented on the Beacon Chain, setting the groundwork for a future shard chain upgrade.

**Phase 2**

Finally, in Phase 2, Ethereum WebAssembly, or eWASM, will be introduced. The World Wide Web Consortium created WebAssembly to make Ethereum significantly more efficient than it is presently. Ethereum WebAssembly is a suggested deterministic subset of WebAssembly for the Ethereum smart contract execution layer. Ethereum currently possesses an Ethereum Virtual Machine, or EVM. Because of an EVM, Ethereum can function as a global supercomputer, and users all over the globe can use it to run smart contracts and interact with decentralized apps (DApps). The EVM stores all the code required to execute Ethereum commands, facilitate transaction wallet addresses, and compute transaction (gas) fees.

The EVM can handle several jobs at the same time. Among these jobs is deciding if a smart contract can be terminated (it consumes too much gas). The determinism of a DApp (whether it constantly executes the same inputs and outputs) and the isolation of a smart contract (its error will not affect the Ethereum network). In contrast, the Ethereum network has gotten overloaded. Because numerous transactions are taking place simultaneously, the EVM is running much slower than expected. Ethereum's EVM is also difficult to update because it was written in Solidity's proprietary, difficult-to-understand language. They developed the eWASM to replace the EVM, which would be implemented in Phase 2.

The eWASM generates code significantly quicker than the EVM, which speeds up network activities. The eWASM makes the Gas function more efficiently, yet it's compatible with standard coding languages like C and C++. The eWASM is intended to make Ethereum development considerably more accessible.

Unfortunately, due to difficulties in executing the previous phases, the introduction of stage two has been severely delayed. When the eWASM goes into action is unknown to developers.

## How to Become a Validator on Ethereum
## Hardware Requirements

Validators are intended to use several infrastructure settings based on Eth2's decentralized design goals (on-premise, cloud, etc.). Below are some hardware suggestions and resource links to help you get ready.

### Recommended Specs:

- Operating Systems: Linux 64-bit, Mac OS X, and Windows
- Intel Core i7-4770 or AMD FX-8310 processor (or better)
- RAM: 8 gigabytes
- Storage: 100GB available space SSD
- Internet: Broadband internet access (10 Mbps)
- Power: Uninterruptible power supply (UPS)
- Digital Ocean Equivalent (cloud provider):

### Minimum Requirements:

- Operating Systems: Linux 64-bit, Mac OS X, and Windows
- Intel Core i5-760 or AMD FX-8110 processor (or better)
- 4GB RAM
- SSD with 20GB of storage space
- Internet: Broadband internet access (10 Mbps)
- Power: Uninterruptible power supply (UPS)

### Choosing and Installing Your Client

With the release of Eth 2.0, validators can now employ alternative implementations when executing their validator. There are four customer teams with production-ready implementations available right now:

### Prysm by Prysmatic Labs (Discord)

Prysm is a Go implementation of Ethereum 2.0 that prioritizes usability, security, and dependability. Prysm is developed in Go and licensed under the GNU General Public License 3.0.

### Lighthouse by Sigma Prime (Discord)

Lighthouse is a Rust implementation of the Eth2.0 client that prioritizes performance and security. Sigma Prime, the company behind it, specializes in information security and software engineering. The Apache 2.0 License applies to Lighthouse.

### Teku by ConsenSys (Discord)

PegaSys Teku is a Java-based Ethereum 2.0 client that was created with institutional needs and security in mind. Teku is an Apache 2 licensed application built in Java, a mature and widely used programming language.

### Nimbus by Status (Discord)

Nimbus is a research project, and Ethereum 2.0 client implementation optimized for embedded systems and personal mobile devices, including outdated cellphones with limited hardware resources. Nimbus (Apache 2) is developed in Nim, a Python-like scripting language that compiles to C.

## Install an ETH 1.0 Node

To watch for 32 ETH validator deposits while running a validator on Eth2, you must also operate an Eth1 node. When it comes to picking an Eth1 node, there are several possibilities. The tools most typically used to spin up an Eth1 node are listed below.

Self-Hosting:

- OpenEthereum
- Geth
- Besu
- Nethermind

## Hosted by a third party:

- Infura

## Running an Eth 2.0 Validator
## Step 1: Get ETH

If you're new to Ethereum, acquiring your fuel to participate is a crucial first step. Each validator in Eth2 requires 32 ETH, and if you decide to become a validator, you'll be committing to this endeavor for a long time (years).

Here are some recommended exchanges if you need to top up on ETH.

- Coinbase or Gemini are two US fiat on-ramp exchanges.
- Binance or Kraken are two non-US fiat on-ramp exchanges.
- Ethereum DEX: Uniswap

**Step 2: Go to Eth2 Launchpad**

The Ethereum Foundation (EF), Codefi Activate, and Deep Work Studio have been developing an interface to make it easier for people to stake and become validators on Ethereum 2.0 over the last several months. The Eth2 LaunchPad is the culmination of this effort. This safe application walks you through establishing your Eth2 key pairs and staking your 32 ETH in the official deposit contract on the Eth2 mainnet. They created the LaunchPad with at-home validators in mind. These computer enthusiasts want to build their validator and are familiar with executing commands in a terminal window.

**Step 3: Create your mnemonic phrase and key pairs**

It would help if you produced a validator key pair and a mnemonic phrase for each validator node to generate your withdrawal key afterward. You must first choose the number of validators you want to run and the operating system you want to run them on.

To produce your deposit keys, the Launchpad will give you two alternatives. The first is to run the deposit command in your terminal window after downloading the binary executable file from the Eth2 Github source. You can build the deposit-CLI utility from the Python source code. Follow the instructions to verify that you have all the essential development libraries and the deposit-CLI tool installed.

When you run the deposit-CLI utility in your terminal window after installing it, you will be requested to:

- Choose the number of validators you want to run.
- Set the language in which you want to create your mnemonic phrase

- Choose the network (mainnet) where you want your validator to execute.

- If you don't provide —a chain mainnet for the Mainnet testnet, the deposit will be invalid.

- You will be prompted to create a password, after which the system produces your mnemonic phrase. Make sure you've written it down and saved it somewhere safe!

## Step 4: Upload your deposit file

You're nearly there. Deposit-data-[timestamp].json may be found in the /eth2.0-deposit-cli/validator keys directory.

## Step 5: Connect your wallet

After that, link your Web3 wallet and click next. Make sure you select Mainnet in your wallet's settings.

## Step 6: Review the transaction summary and begin the deposit

After you've connected and validated your wallet address, the system will lead you to a summary page that shows the total amount of ETH you'll need to transfer to the deposit contract based on how many validators you've chosen to run. Accept the alert checks and click accept to proceed to the next step, the actual deposit. Click ' Initiate Transaction' to deposit your ETH into the official Eth2 Deposit Contract. The 32 ETH deposit per validator must be confirmed using your wallet. When your transaction has been confirmed, Boom! You've done it, and you can now call yourself an official staker for a historic Web3 event.

## Promising Changes by Ethereum 2.0

The following five modifications will be implemented in Ethereum 2.0:

### Lower Transaction Fees

High gas transaction fees are now Ethereum's central problem. The gas fee is a payment made to miners to validate transactions using their processing capacity. It is expressed in "gwei" and varies depending on network demand. When there is a significant demand for transactions, the Ethereum blockchain is typically blocked. Miners would prioritize transaction requests with higher gas fees in this situation, resulting in a higher overall gas transaction charge. When Ethereum shifts to a PoS proof-of-stake method, processing transactions will become easier, preventing unprocessed transactions from cluttering the network.

### Increase Network Throughput

The inclusion of "sharding" is part of the Ethereum 2.0 update. The blockchain gets sharded into numerous chains that may execute transactions independently of the main chain. PoW blockchains, such as the Bitcoin blockchain, store transactions on an entire chain, including the transaction history since the genesis block was mined in 2009. The amount of transactions that you can execute on a chain, on the other hand, is restricted. Only seven transactions per second are possible with Bitcoin, whereas only 10-15 transactions per second are possible with Ethereum.

On top of the existing primary chain, sharding will construct additional chains. According to the Ethereum Foundation, the sharding mechanism separates the Ethereum blockchain into 64 distinct chains.

The pressure on the Ethereum main network will decrease, and the entire ecosystem's throughput will considerably increase because the system will use different chains to validate transactions.

## Reduce Hardware Requirements

Satoshi Nakamoto wanted everyone to be a member of the transaction verification and recording system when he created Bitcoin. However, changes in the system have raised the bar for regular individuals to engage in network verification. The increase in mining difficulty necessitates the purchase of expensive modern machines to ensure computational power, and Ethereum is experiencing a similar issue. Furthermore, nodes must keep a copy of the blockchain records, which needs nodes to store about 4TB of data and a PC with more than 4TB of storage costs around a few thousand dollars at current market rates. The high cost of software makes it difficult to recruit additional competent verifiers to assist in network protection and construction.

With the advent of the PoS consensus mechanism in Ethereum, validators no longer require specialized computer equipment and may instead rely on server-level technology to validate transactions. Additionally, sharding will lower the amount of disk space needed to keep the Ethereum blockchain's history. The validator only has to record the history of one of the shard chains, which is 1/64 of the total data, because Ethereum will have 64 shard chains in the future.

## Expand The Ethereum Ecosystem

You can use Ethereum's programmability to develop smart contracts and decentralized apps (dApps) that power sectors like NFTs and DeFi and operate as a money settlement mechanism. The Ethereum EVM is a supercomputer that runs on the Ethereum network's various computers (nodes). The EVM holds the code that lets users interact with dApps and executes smart contracts. Even though the EVM has substantially improved Ethereum's network capabilities, its utility has fallen in recent years owing to increased demand in the ecosystem. The number of dApps operating on Ethereum's network has grown dramatically since its inception in 2015, including games (Axie Infinity, CryptoKitties), DeFi protocols (Uniswap, Yearn), and DAO (MakerDAO) among them.

The network processing performance dropped substantially as the load on the EVM increased. However, because the code is written in Solidity, a complicated programming language, developing the EVM is challenging. The Ethereum Web Assembly (eWASM), created by the World Wide Web Consortium to replace the EVM, will be included in Ethereum 2.0, according to prominent actors in the Ethereum network's development.

Other simpler coding languages, such as C++ and Rust, are supported by eWASM. Furthermore, they developed eWASM to comply with current web standards, making it easy to use in standard browsers. Users will be able to access dApps from the browser without the need for browser extensions. The most significant advantage of eWASM is its influence on the developer ecosystem; with more language possibilities, more developers will flock to Ethereum, further encouraging innovation and creativity.

**Reduce Carbon Footprint**

The switch to a PoS proof-of-stake consensus method on Ethereum will cut power usage and positively influence the environment. Indeed, environmentalists and authorities have expressed worry about the energy-intensive nature of PoW proof-of-work systems like Bitcoin and Ethereum 1.0. According to the Ethereum official site, PoS will lower Ethereum's power usage by 90-95 percent. Other scaling options, including rollup and sharding, will reduce the total energy cost of transactions by increasing the network's economies of scale.

## Keys to Unlocking Ethereum 2.0
## New frontiers

It's vital to remember that not all Eth 2.0 stake possibilities are created equal. Custodial and noncustodial staking services are available. This implies that the validator key is either produced and retained by the service provider or the investor. Not your keys, not your coins are a famous crypto rallying cry, and Eth 2.0 is no exception. Knowing who has access to your keys is the same as knowing who has access to your cash, and it is the most crucial aspect of validator setup.

You establish four keys when you deposit funds in Eth 2.0: a public and private validator key set and public and private withdrawal key set. Your automobile key is the validator key. The key "signs on-chain actively" (ETH2 operations such as block proposals and attestations). It's also known as the signature key, and it's constantly available (unless you stop validating by exiting the network). If someone steals the key, you risk missing attestations and facing several fines.

Your secure key is the withdrawal key, and it has authority over the 32 ETH invested in the Eth 2.0 deposit contract and the prizes from network validation. While the validator key is deemed "hot," you can hold the withdrawal in cold storage until deposits open in Phase 1.5

for added security. If you lose your withdrawal key, you'll lose all your money. The user may control the destiny of their investments using decentralized staking. You never hand up your keys to another person. The trade-off is the technical risk, which is entirely your responsibility. Put another way, you need to know what you're doing on a technical level. For example, it's on you if you deposit to the wrong contract.

You might not have the internet access or technical know-how to authenticate the Beacon Chain. Fortunately, there are alternatives: At least 30 staking providers exist, including well-known exchanges like Coinbase and Kraken.

## Staking-As-A-Service

Most controlled exchanges, such as Coinbase and Kraken, provide custodial staking. To participate, you must deposit at least 32 ethers and allow them to set up a validator on your behalf. They also keep track of your validator key. Custodial services have a place, but they have a different risk profile because of their centralized form. When you validate with a service, you're confident in them to run your setup effectively and stick to the initial stake agreements.

Although the convenience of staking with a custodial agency is always appealing, you must accept a new set of dangers. One of the first validators to be cut after the debut of the Beacon Chain was a staking service. The difference in network participation rates and penalties between custodial and noncustodial node services is a general trend worth following. While custodial services will most certainly have more reliable setups, users who went at the time of setting up a device themselves are likely to have a higher level of passion for Eth 2.0 as a project, which might translate to better maintenance in the future.

**Key Takeaways**

- Proof-of-work was the initial approach used by Bitcoin for blockchain consensus. Miners, who give their computer processing power, such as graphics processing units (GPUs) and central processing units (CPUs), perform complex algorithms and validate blocks in the PoW system.

- The gas fee is a payment made to miners to validate transactions using their processing capacity. When there is a significant demand for transactions, the Ethereum blockchain is typically blocked. Miners would prioritize transaction requests with higher gas fees in this situation, resulting in a higher overall gas transaction charge. When Ethereum shifts to a PoS proof-of-stake method, processing transactions will become easier, preventing unprocessed transactions from cluttering the network.

- The inclusion of "sharding" is part of the Ethereum 2.0 update. The blockchain gets sharded into numerous chains that may execute transactions independently of the main chain.

- Custodial and noncustodial staking services are available. This implies that the validator key is either produced and retained by the service provider or the investor.

# CHAPTER 2

## ETHEREUM MINING

### Cryptocurrency Mining

Cryptocurrency mining entails allocating computational resources to the solution of complex arithmetic problems. Because there are numerous miners on the network, the first one to tackle the problem will be awarded new ETH currencies for creating the next block. Proof of Work mining is the name of this sort of mining (PoW).

In the Ethereum network, mining also entails checking and validating transactions. Before a transaction can be stored in the blockchain, it must be validated. Miners are paid transaction fees in exchange for their efforts. To have their transactions listed on the blockchain, both ordinary users and smart contracts must pay network fees.

There are three sorts of incentives for Ethereum miners:

- Block rewards – the money given to miners in exchange for creating a new block;
- Transaction fees — the money given to miners to encourage them to verify transactions;
- Gas fees- are similar to transaction fees, except they are paid via smart contracts.

## Introduction to Ethereum Mining

One of the most common methods to invest in Ethereum is through mining. It is the process of allocating computational resources to transaction verification and the generation of new Ethereum blocks. It also requires adding to the network's governance and security.

Ethereum is a decentralized, self-contained blockchain network made up of three parties:

- Developers
- Miners
- Users

The developers write the code and make the necessary adjustments to the network. Miners assist in creating new coins, the confirmation of transactions, and the administration of the blockchain. Users make use of the network's selling offer. In the case of Ethereum, it is a smart contract platform. Smart contracts are bits of code that run on their own when specific criteria are satisfied, and they use Ethereum's distributed computing network.

Ethereum also offers Ether (ETH), a decentralized digital currency that you can use to facilitate value exchange inside the network or on cryptocurrency exchanges. The three aspects of the Ethereum network are interconnected, and they must always function in unison. It will fail if the developers cease adding to the network, and if miners cease mining or users depart the community, the same thing happens.

## Ethereum Mining Mechanism

As previously noted, Ethereum relies on the well-known PoW consensus algorithm to support block creation. This method has both advantages and disadvantages. However, according to the Ethereum core developers, it appears to have more disadvantages than advantages. The major drawback is that it is not scalable in its current form. Other decentralized apps (dApps) can operate on Ethereum's network because it is a Turing Complete blockchain. It must be accomplished quickly to do this. To address this issue, engineers have upgraded the network to Ethereum 2.0, which uses the Proof of Stake (PoS) consensus process. To protect and grow the network, PoS employs staking rather than mining.

## Ethereum's Proof of Work

There are two components of PoW mining that you must comprehend. These are the following:

## Hashrate

This is the number of calculations that all computers (miners) in the network can complete in a single second, measured in hashes per second (H/s). This implies that the greater the hash rate, the more miners there are on the network, and vice versa.

## Network difficulty

You measure this in hashes per solution, and it's a metric for how complicated mathematical problems are to solve.

The two variables are inextricably linked to one another. The network's difficulty follows the hash rate, increasing (or decreasing) in the hash rate, causing an increase (or reduction) in the difficulty score.

When it comes to managing block creation time, network difficulties are crucial. The network generates Ethereum's blocks every 14 seconds, and the problem automatically changes as this number grows or decreases.

## Ethereum Mining Methods

You can mine Ethereum (and any other cryptocurrency that supports a PoW consensus) in three different methods. They are as follows:

### Solo Mining

This involves mining alone. There are no mining pools to join, no partnerships to form. The notion is that the miner may use his or her hashing resources to actively contribute to the solution of mathematical problems and the verification of transactions. Unless you can build up an industrial-grade mining operation, mining Ethereum alone is strongly discouraged. The hash rate necessary to mine a block on Ethereum has surpassed that of a hobbyist, and anyone attempting to mine alone may have to wait a long time to see any results.

### Pool Mining

Pool mining entails joining a group of miners and contributing one's hashing power to a shared pool. When miners join forces, their total hashing rate rises, enhancing their chances of producing the next block. Not all pools, however, are advised. When looking for a mining pool to join, keep the following elements in mind:

- Location: Join a mining pool as close as possible to you.
- The size of the pool. The larger the mining pool, the greater the overall hash rate, which means you can create more blocks.
- The smallest possible distribution. You'd want to obtain your money as quickly as possible. The smaller the minimum payout amount, the sooner you'll be able to reap the benefits of your mining efforts.
- Fees for using the pool. This usually falls between 0.5 and 1.5 percent, which is the fee of becoming a pool member. The smaller the fees, the better, but this is not always the case. You should also evaluate the other considerations and decide what is appropriate for your scenario.

## Cloud Mining

This is similar to pool mining, except that you donate money instead of donating hashing power. The network uses the funds to acquire Ethereum mining equipment, which will be mined on your behalf by the cloud mining company. The profits are distributed evenly to all investors, with the firm getting a fee for its services.

## Advantages of Cloud Mining

Here are some reasons why you might consider investing in a cloud mining company:

- Purchase, install and maintain the equipment instead. This is a fantastic benefit of cloud mining. Most people who want to mine Ethereum aren't technically savvy; thus, having to outsource this task may be enticing.

- It's easier and less expensive to start and run. Continuing from the previous point, the investor would avoid Ethereum mining disadvantages such as noise from the GPU cooling fans by using cloud mining. During operation, GPUs frequently overheat. However, you won't have to worry about getting rid of the worn-out miners.

Disadvantages of Cloud Mining

Cloud mining has several drawbacks, including:

- Control over the mining equipment is lacking. Investors in cloud mining sometimes have little control over how their equipment is used. You can repurpose GPUs to mine currencies other than Ethereum, and investors may have no idea what coins their equipment is mining.

- For investors, it's too risky. In this business model, the risk-to-reward ratio is skewed adversely in favor of investors, with little to no risk taken by the company's operators.

- Scams. This business concept is popular with scammers.

**Implication for Ethereum Miners**

Mining ethereum is not as profitable as most of 2021 due to the current price slump. Depending on local energy prices, a single Nvidia 3080 may still make around $3.50 per day mining Ethereum, half the profit of late 2021. Even if the value of Ethereum rises again, the merger will put a stop to profitable mining.

The difficulty bomb will effectively render Ethereum mining useless, forcing anybody presently mining the token to switch to another coin or sell their graphics cards in favor of staking. You can mine other Proof of Work cryptocurrencies for a profit with consumer gear, but these alternatives may not be viable with so many Ethereum miners looking for new coins to mine. Let's explore why it'll be tough to continue mining cryptocurrencies successfully unless substantial fluctuations in the popularity of particular coins occur.

Although Ethereum 2.0 is not yet complete, the final stages will reduce ETH mining. The "merge" phase will mark the end of proof-of-work mining and the termination of mining incentives for users. There will also be no miner extractable value (MEV) (The profit a miner (or validator, sequencer, etc.) may gain by arbitrarily including, excluding, or re-ordering transactions inside the blocks they create). However, there are speculations about new ways of doing things which will be very profitable to the Ethereum community.

**Ethereum 2.0 Investment**

We will eliminate mining rewards by switching to a proof-of-stake consensus mechanism. The "burn rate" (the number of tokens burnt instead of being given to miners) may exceed how new currencies are generated. Ethereum burned $14 million worth of ETH in only two days after issuing EIP 1559 instead of paying validators. If the current burn rate continues, ETH supply will be constrained, potentially driving up the price. From this perspective, it appears like ETH 2.0 will generate value.

However, it will be impossible to profit from ETH until the ultimate release of Ethereum 2.0. As the complexity of solving puzzles increases, mining profits will plummet. In March 2021, the difficulty of mining ETH reached an all-time high of 6,000 Terahash. Mining will no longer depend on the anonymous competition after the merger, and users must invest part of their ETH in validating newly generated tokens. As a result, it will reduce ETH liquidity.

The platform will not permit staked ETH withdrawal before the introduction of ETH2.0, preventing users from investing their ETH in other apps. However, all of these changes are public information and should have already been included in the price of ETH. Furthermore, if the project sees the light of day and proves to be helpful in scalability and sustainability, other cryptocurrencies, such as Bitcoin, may follow suit and adopt a proof-of-stake consensus.

**Key Takeaways**

- Ethereum mining is the process of allocating computational resources to transaction verification and the generation of new Ethereum blocks.

- There are three sorts of incentives for Ethereum miners: Block rewards - money given to miners in exchange for creating a new block; Transaction fees — the money given to miners to encourage them to verify transactions; Gas fees- are similar to transaction fees, except they are paid via smart contracts.

- Ethereum (and any other cryptocurrency that supports a Proof of work consensus) may be mined in three different methods.

**They are as follows:**

**Solo mining** involves mining alone, and there are no joining mining pools, no partnerships to form.

**Pool mining** entails joining a group of miners and contributing one's hashing power to a shared pool.

**Cloud mining** is similar to pool mining, except that you donate money instead of donating hashing power.

- Although Ethereum 2.0 is not yet complete, the final stages will reduce ETH mining. The "merge" phase will mark the end of proof-of-work mining and the termination of mining incentives for users. There will also be no miners extractable value (MEV).

# CHAPTER 3

## BUYING AND SELLING IN ETHEREUM 2.0

**Quick Steps to Buy Ethereum**

You'll need to register a trading account with a crypto broker or a recognized crypto exchange if you want to acquire cryptocurrencies in 2022. Follow the four steps below to understand how to buy Ethereum through the SEC-regulated broker eToro.

**Step 1: Signup for an eToro account.**

To begin, create an account. You to supply contact information, personal information, and a copy of your ID to eToro.

**Step 2: Make a deposit**

Next, make a deposit to cover the cost of your Ethereum investment. Online banking, debit/credit cards, and e-wallets are all accepted payment options. For US consumers, the minimum deposit is only $10.

**Step 3: Search for Ethereum**

Use the search box at the top of the page to look for 'Ethereum.' Click the 'Trade' button when you see ETH appear.

**Step 4: Buy Ethereum**

Finally, input your stake and click 'Open Trade' to purchase Ethereum.

It will deduct your account balance, and add the ETH tokens to your portfolio in seconds.

**Best Platforms to Buy Ethereum in 2022**

When learning how to buy Ethereum, you must first decide which cryptocurrency platform to use to conduct your transaction.

To help you navigate the haze, here is a list of the top exchanges to buy Ethereum.

**eToro**

eToro platform is appropriate for both novices and experienced traders because you will have access to a regulated and low-cost trading environment. In terms of the former, eToro is licensed by several tier-one regulatory authorities, including the SEC, FCA, CySEC, and ASIC.

eToro, on the other hand, is a spread-only broker, which means there are no set commissions. All fee-free USD deposits and withdrawals are another cost-effective feature of the eToro platform. This includes debit and credit card payments, which often have a 3-5 percent transaction charge in the bitcoin exchange sector. You may buy Ethereum via a bank transfer, ACH, or an e-wallet like PayPal in addition to debit/credit cards.

The network will add the tokens to your online wallet once you have made your Ethereum investment - which needs a minimum capital outlay of just $10 at eToro. You do not have to make a withdrawal if you leave the tokens there. This implies that when the time comes to convert your Ethereum tokens to actual currency, you may do it with the click of a button. In terms of diversity, eToro is our top choice.

You can purchase Bitcoin and 40+ other cryptocurrencies, like Polkadot, Binance Coin, the Graph, XRP, Shiba Inu, and dozens of different markets through the broker. All included stocks listed in the United States and on more than a dozen foreign exchanges and ETFs, gold, energies, indexes, and currencies. Finally, the eToro copy trading tool is worth looking at. This allows you to choose a prominent eToro trader and then mimic their investments in the future.

You may, for example, acquire the Graph currency with a minimum spread of just 2.9 percent because of the narrow spreads. eToro is especially famous among crypto lovers since it provides a sound cryptocurrency credit card.

### Crypto.com

Crypto.com is the another exchange to consider when looking for a place to purchase Ethereum. It offers a wide range of other crypto-related products and services; this platform is more than simply an exchange. Crypto.com, for example, has an NFT marketplace where you can buy NFTs using Ethereum, as well as the option to earn interest on your cryptocurrency investments and even a Visa-issued debit card.

When purchasing Ethereum on Crypto.com, utilizing your Visa or MasterCard is the fastest way. Your transaction will be completed immediately as a result of this. However, you should be aware that Crypto.com imposes a fixed transaction cost of 2.99 percent when using this payment method. If you're a new client, this cost is waived for the first 30 days after registering an account.

Crypto.com is similar to eToro in that it was created with novices in mind. The user experience is simple and easy to use on both the main website and the iOS/Android mobile app. Furthermore, opening an account is simple, and the KYC verification procedure takes less than two minutes. We also appreciate that Crypto.com allows crypto loans, has over 250 different cryptocurrencies on its site, and regularly introduces new tokens.

## Binance

While eToro and Crypto.com are ideal for beginners, Binance is undoubtedly the finest site for buying Ethereum if you've used a cryptocurrency exchange before. You may trade on Binance's sophisticated platform, which offers you access to several features that seasoned investors would enjoy. This features advanced orders, customizable charts, technical indicators, and sketching tools, among other things.

When purchasing Ethereum on Binance, you may use a debit or credit card to pay for your tokens right away. If you want to deposit funds in US dollars, you must first go through a brief KYC procedure. Furthermore, if you use a debit or credit card on this site, you will be charged a hefty 4.5 percent fee and a usual buy fee of 0.5 percent. Binance, on the other hand, accepts fee-free ACH and bank wire transfers; however, you must wait for the money to clear before purchasing ETH.

Another option for purchasing Ethereum on Binance is to make a cryptocurrency deposit. This will expedite the KYC verification procedure, but you will also avoid paying any deposit costs. Furthermore, Binance offers many Ethereum-denominated trading pairs, allowing you to pay for your purchase using USDT, Bitcoin, or Binance Coin. If you choose a crypto-to-Ethereum exchange, you'll pay an industry-low fee of only 0.10 percent for each slide.

Furthermore, Binance accepts a broad range of cryptocurrencies, allowing you to purchase Celo and other popular altcoins with some of the lowest transaction fees available.

**Coinbase**

Coinbase is the best of both worlds in terms of user-friendliness and security. In terms of the former, Coinbase is frequently the first pick for consumers looking to purchase Ethereum for the first time, not least since the platform was designed with beginners in mind. Coinbase requires no prior bitcoin trading knowledge, and you can create verified accounts within 10 minutes.

Coinbase is regulated in the United States, and you can trade it publicly on the NASDAQ exchange. All registered users must go through a KYC procedure, and the platform retains at least 98 percent of customer cash in cold storage. Each account login attempt also requires two-factor authentication. Although Coinbase is excellent for novices and security, it has one major flaw: its deposits and commissions are pretty costly.

When you purchase and sell Ethereum here, regular charges of 1.49 percent will be applied. And, if you want to utilize Coinbase's Instant

Buy option, which accepts debit/credit cards and Paypal, you'll have to pay an additional 3.99 percent. It would help if you also accounted for the spread and withdrawal costs, which vary by payment type. Finally, Coinbase provides more than 50 marketplaces if you want to acquire Ethereum and other digital tokens.

## Ethereum Payment Options

If you want to purchase Ethereum right now but aren't sure which payment method to use, look at the options below.

### Credit or Debit Card

Using a credit or debit card is the most convenient way to purchase Ethereum. Here's how to complete the procedure in a few minutes and avoid having to pay any deposit fees:

- Sign up for an eToro account.
- Choose a debit/credit card from the list of deposit options.
- Make a fee-free deposit of at least $10.

It's worth noting that eToro is one of the few cryptocurrency exchanges that will let you purchase Ethereum using a credit or debit card without incurring any fees. For example, Coinbase costs 3.99 percent, whereas Binance charges 4.5 percent.

### PayPal

Consider purchasing Ethereum using PayPal as an alternative. You may deposit cash at the popular exchange Coinbase using PayPal, but you'll have to pay 3.99 percent of the transaction value again, and the cost is higher if the purchase is less than $200.

Alternatively, you may purchase Ethereum using PayPal at eToro and avoid paying any costs.

**Choosing an Ethereum Wallet**

After you've figured out how to acquire Ethereum and where to do it, the last thing to think about is storage. After all, Ethereum tokens are kept in digital wallets, and Ethereum wallets are available in various forms, including mobile apps, desktop applications, and hardware devices. Choose cautiously since each Ethereum wallet will provide a unique combination of security and convenience.

Beginners may enjoy the user-friendly features of the eToro Money Crypto Wallet if they are unsure which solution is ideal for them. This Ethereum wallet is available as a mobile app and allows you to store your tokens safely and for free.

Furthermore, the Gibraltar Financial Services Commission has granted the wallet a license. You will be able to keep your tokens in the eToro Money Crypto Wallet, but you will also be able to sell them back for US dollars at any moment.

**How to Cash Out Ethereum**

You may trade one coin for another on a cryptocurrency exchange. When you cash out Ethereum, you exchange your cryptocurrency for fiat currency (usually Dollars or Euros). The most frequent way to pay out Ethereum is to sell it on a cryptocurrency exchange for cash. To cash out your Ethereum, follow these seven steps:

- Choose a cryptocurrency exchange.

- Link an existing bank account.

- Send your Ethereum to a cryptocurrency exchange.

- Transfer your mining profits to a cryptocurrency exchange.

- Exchange your Ethereum into the desired currency.

- Take money out of your bank account.

- Pay the costs for withdrawals.

## How to Sell Ethereum

The most frequent way to receive fiat dollars for your Ethereum is to sell it on a crypto exchange. However, you may sell your Ethereum to other people and receive dollars or euros. You may accomplish this by putting up a private ad to state your desire to sell your Ethereum. You can also utilize peer-to-peer networks. These alternatives put you in direct contact with the buyer, enabling you to select a price and schedule a face-to-face meeting with your buyer to complete the transaction. You are interacting with individuals when you choose peer-to-peer trading. The odds of your transaction going wrong are much larger.

## Three tips for Selling Ethereum

Here are a few pointers to keep in mind while selling Ethereum directly.

- Keep a watch out for con artists.

You'll need active internet connectivity to finalize the purchase when meeting with a peer buyer. Before you confirm a transaction on your end, ensure sure the individual with whom you're dealing has the funds and is willing to finalize the transaction on their end. People have been known to push the send button at the exact moment.

- Make every effort to avoid making mistakes.

Always check the public addresses, the amount you're transferring, and the current exchange rate before proceeding.

- Take precautions.

When scheduling a face-to-face encounter, ensure that you meet in a public location and take all required procedures to protect your physical safety.

**Investing in Ethereum Stocks**

There are various methods to benefit from Ethereum's expanding popularity. The most straightforward way is to purchase Ethereum. This poses the highest risk and the biggest possible returns due to its extraordinary volatility, and Ethereum stocks are a less volatile choice. Managed funds that invest in Ethereum on your behalf and organizations with significant exposure to Ethereum technology are examples.

These are the best stocks to buy if you want to add Ethereum exposure to your portfolio:

## Grayscale Ethereum Trust

The Grayscale Ethereum Trust (OTC: ETHE) is a managed fund that allows you to add Ethereum to your brokerage account quickly. Each share is backed by a predetermined number of Ether tokens (approximately 0.01 Ether per share). Keep in mind that the fund's share price is frequently less than the current value of Ethereum. Grayscale also charges a somewhat high annual management fee of 2.5 percent. Price arbitrage is impossible since shareholders cannot exchange their shares for Ethereum.

## Bitwise Ethereum Fund

Bitwise is the largest crypto index fund manager in the world, and it provides managed funds for various cryptocurrencies, including the Bitwise Ethereum Fund. A minimum commitment of $25,000 is required to participate in this fund, which is only open to authorized investors. The fund's management aims to reduce transaction costs by storing its Ethereum in cold crypto storage, making it a cost-effective and safe Ethereum stock. It charges a 1.5 percent yearly management fee.

## Coinbase

Coinbase (NASDAQ: COIN) is the United States' largest cryptocurrency exchange. The firm charges buyers and sellers of various cryptocurrencies, including Ethereum, transaction fees. Many of the other cryptocurrencies traded on Coinbase, in addition to Ethereum, utilize the Ethereum blockchain. Coinbase has witnessed explosive growth as more people turn to bitcoin, making it one of the most lucrative cryptocurrency stocks. Monthly users increased by 487 percent from 1.5 million in the second quarter of 2020 to 8.8 million a year later. Over the same time, net revenue increased by more than 1,000 percent, from $178 million to $2.03 billion.

## Staked ETH Trust

Ethereum is currently undergoing an upgrade to Ethereum 2.0. Switching to a proof-of-stake approach to validate transactions is part of that process. Ether token holders may stake crypto in this model to be used to validate transactions and receive rewards.

The Staked ETH Trust is the first regular investment vehicle to provide owners with Ethereum exposure and staking incentives. Accredited investors can invest in the fund through a private placement. It has a $25,000 minimum investment requirement and a 1% expense ratio.

## HIVE Blockchain

HIVE Blockchain (TSXV: HIVE) is a firm that specializes in bitcoin mining. It mines bitcoin using green energy facilities, utilizing computational power to validate transactions and collect incentives. Bitcoin, Ethereum, and Ethereum Classic are the three cryptocurrencies it presently mines (CRYPTO: ETC).

It's worth mentioning that, while HIVE has previously concentrated on Ethereum, this is likely to alter in the future. The cryptocurrency will move away from the proof-of-work architecture and Ethereum mining it has been using to confirm transactions when it upgrades to Ethereum 2.0. It is switching to a proof-of-stake approach that does not include crypto mining.

For the time being, HIVE is a technique to obtain Ethereum exposure, but after the Ethereum 2.0 launch, it will shift its attention to other proof-of-work cryptocurrencies.

## Tech Companies Building on Ethereum

At the height of the 2017 ICO bubble, when Bitcoin hit over $20,000 (and Ethereum didn't fair so badly, peaking at $1,432, according to CoinMarketCap), many firms began looking into Ethereum. Some of the world's largest firms use Ethereum, including video game company Ubisoft, Dutch bank ING, and TD Ameritrade.

### Ubisoft

Ubisoft, a French video game publisher, is responsible for some of the world's most popular triple-A gaming series, including Assassin's Creed, Far Cry, and Watch Dogs. It has embraced blockchain significantly, investing in eight blockchain firms through its Entrepreneur Lab and collaborating on the game Nine Chronicles with blockchain games company Planetarium.

It's no surprise, therefore, that Ubisoft is using Ethereum as well. Based on its famous Raving Rabbids series, Rabbids Tokens were released a few months ago. Rabbids Tokens are based on Ethereum's ERC-721 token standard, created by the same team that brought you CryptoKitties; each non-fungible token (NFT) depicts one of Ubisoft's frightening cartoon bunnies.

The tokens were used in a game where you deposit money into an Ethereum wallet and then use it to "nab" (purchase) a Rabbid from another user. Upon purchase, the token will begin to represent another

Rabbids character, and the network records the entire transaction in your virtual logbook.

**Key Takeaways**

- You'll need to register a trading account with a crypto broker or a recognized crypto exchange if you want to acquire cryptocurrencies in 2022.

- When learning how to buy Ethereum, you must first decide which cryptocurrency platform to use to conduct your transaction. There are a host of platforms to choose from.

- After you've figured out how to acquire Ethereum and where to do it, the last thing to think about is storage. After all, Ethereum tokens are kept in digital wallets.

- Ethereum wallets are available in various forms, including mobile apps, desktop applications, and hardware devices. Choose cautiously since each Ethereum wallet will provide a unique combination of security and convenience.

- The most frequent way to receive fiat dollars for your Ethereum is to sell it on a crypto exchange. However, you may sell your Ethereum to other people and receive dollars or euros. You may accomplish this by putting up a private ad to state your desire to sell your Ethereum. You can also utilize peer-to-peer networks. These alternatives put you in direct contact with the buyer, enabling you to select a price and schedule a face-to-face meeting with your buyer to complete the transaction. You are interacting with individuals when you choose peer-to-peer trading. The odds of your transaction going wrong are much larger.

- There are several methods to benefit from Ethereum's expanding popularity. The most straightforward way is to purchase Ethereum. This poses the highest risk and the biggest possible returns due to its extraordinary volatility, but Ethereum stocks are a less volatile choice.

# CHAPTER 4

## ETHEREUM 2.0 AND ETHEREUM CRYPTOCURRENCY

The blockchain that underpins Ether, the second-largest cryptocurrency, will soon receive a much-anticipated update, resulting in more institutional investors investing in the network, helping boost Ether's price.

The objective is to make Ethereum, the improved blockchain, more scalable, safe, and long-lasting. It would, among other things, render crypto mining obsolete, decreasing the enormous amount of energy necessary to generate new currencies, which has been a cause of fierce criticism.

**Effect on Ethereum Cryptocurrency**
**Less Energy Used**

Ethereum currently employs proof-of-work, which forces miners to solve complex puzzles to validate transactions and create a new currency. This technology requires a substantial amount of computer processing power, and it has been criticized for harming the environment. Ethereum will transition to proof-of-stake, allowing users to confirm transactions depending on the number of tokens they donate or stake. Users who stake more coins have a better chance of being chosen to validate network transactions and earning a reward.

Ethereum is now operating two chains in parallel: proof-of-work and proof-of-stake. While both chains include validators, only the proof-of-work chain currently performs user transactions. Once the integration is complete, Ethereum's blockchain will be entirely replaced by the Beacon Network, a proof-of-stake chain that will render mining useless.

As a result, we expect Ethereum's energy usage to be reduced by 99 percent. Due to the lower environmental effect, we expect more institutional investors to acquire Ether, use its blockchain, invest in its network, and increase adoption. Ethereum engineers successfully tested the update as part of final preparations for the integration, boosting optimism about the upgrade's possibilities.

## Price Increase

Following the "merge," the quantity of Ether is projected to decrease as fewer tokens are likely to be created. Following the merger, we expect the amount of ETH produced to shrink by 90%, resulting in comparable fees reducing Ether's supply by 5% a year. The price of Ether may climb if demand rises while supply falls; however, it is difficult to anticipate the cost of any asset in the future. Following the merger, some believe Ether will become a deflationary asset or one with a diminishing supply that you can use as a value store. Bitcoin is already regarded as a haven asset.

## Possible High Return

Validators will "stake," or contribute, their Ether to crypto wallets under proof-of-stake. Since mining will become obsolete under the new proof-of-stake architecture, fees that were previously given to miners for their efforts will become somewhat of a passive income for validators.

**Key Takeaways**

- The objective of Ethereum 2.0 is to make the blockchain more scalable, safe, and long-lasting.

- We expect Ethereum's energy usage to be reduced by 99 percent when Ethereum 2.0 launches. Due to the lower environmental effect, more institutional investors are expected to acquire Ether, use its blockchain, invest in its network, and increase adoption.

- After the "merge," the quantity of Ether is projected to decrease as fewer tokens are likely to be created, which will likely lead to an increase in the price of Ethereum.

# CHAPTER 5

## ETHEREUM 2.0 MEGATRENDS

### Banking and Ethereum 2.0 Staking

Banks may play an essential role in Ethereum 2.0 in the future. According to Blockdaemon and Bison Trails, who provide the infrastructure to allow hosting a staking node on Ethereum 2.0, low risk and easy to install, it's a trend that will soon attract as much attention as institutional investment in bitcoin. The number of giant firms eager to participate in Ethereum's next-generation network has astonished these intermediaries in the staking area. When traditional savings vehicles yield pitiful returns, the network's proof-of-stake (PoS) system gives incentives equivalent to interest, priced in Ether (ETH).

### Institutional Staking

Unlike Bitcoin's energy-intensive crypto mining technology, which is now under fire from critics, the next generation of blockchain networks use Proof of Stake (PoS), in which blocks of transactions are added to the chain by a consensus of persons who individually own tokens on the network. Validators who stake their tokens on the network gain a reward but risk losing a portion of their stake (slashing) if they do not act consistently. Several proof-of-stake blockchains include Polkadot, Cardano, and Algorand, but Ethereum's move away from proof-of-work is the most anxiously anticipated. Ethereum 2.0 is a huge thing, and the changeover will make keeping ETH in a wallet and collecting income as straightforward as keeping a bank account. All you need is an ETH wallet, and it will generate interest on its own.

**Proof of Swiss**

Crypto-friendly Switzerland has made the most progress in giving institutional staking. Digital asset bank Sygnum is now enabling Ethereum 2.0 staking. Sygnum isn't new to staking: a few months ago, the crypto bank gave its asset management, hedge fund, and family office customers the option to stake on the Tezos network.

Sygnum's Ethereum staking service will include locking up multiples of 32 ETH for an unspecified amount of time until Ethereum 2.0 launch. According to Thomas Eichenberger, head of business units at Sygnum Bank, this will yield between 8% and 6.5 percent every year.

"Given its market value and the network's prominence, Ethereum is attracting a lot of interest from institutional customers who aren't necessarily familiar with the entire ecosystem but want to start with some of the bigger currencies," Eichenberger said in an interview.

**Ethereum's Triple Halving**

So, what exactly is Ethereum halving? Three key pillars lie at the center of this debate.

- Cost of mining coins due to energy usage
- Coin value and inflation
- The connection between "proof of work" and "proof of stake."

So let's take a closer look at "proof of work" and "proof of stake."

Let's start using Bitcoin to accomplish so:

The bitcoin network uses the Proof of Work principle to authorize BTC or Bitcoin. This implies that you must solve mathematical encryption or problem before you can transfer money from one account to another. This strategy, however, has certain drawbacks. Due to the highly energy-intensive nature of mining coins, it drains computational resources and delays transactions. There are environmental problems, but PoW also demands a growing amount of time for every puzzle, making blockchain sluggish and inefficient in critical scenarios like price volatility. In terms of authorization, Ethereum was formerly the same. However, the introduction of DeFi in recent years has given rise to a variety of new use cases for financial decentralization. Users, developers, investors, and purchasers have all expressed a desire for a different type of authorization that uses less power, reduces volatility, and enhances security.

As a result, Ethereum has begun its path to Ethereum 2.0. This is where Ethereum's triple halving comes into play. They developed Ethereum 2.0 mainly to overcome the scalability challenges that prevent widespread cryptocurrency adoption by providing more incentives than ever before to individuals (and users). If you're a member of the Ether network with some stakes stored up, you'll also get rewarded.

Triple halving is a new protocol that shifts consensus away from intensive proof-of-work and toward proof-of-stake in Ethereum blockchain coins. Instead of rewarding blocks with the most processing power, you'll receive a 1% share for every ETH token you hold when creating and submitting your block, regardless of how much computational power they represent. It will also let you participate in liquidity pools with your stake, allowing you to profit from numerous DeFi protocols on your chain.

It brought a significant modification in the form of EIP-1559 via an Ethereum update on August 5, 2021, known as the London hard fork. EIP 1559 is a programming modification that takes some ETH out of circulation. EIP-1559 will alter the way you calculate transaction fees. The effect is that everybody who initiates a transaction on the network will now pay a basic fee that will be burnt rather than going to Ethereum miners. In this context, burning involves removing money from circulation by sending them to an address where no one has the keys.

If you reduce the supply of Eth, the Ethereum network will experience "deflationary pressure." While new currencies will be minted with each block added to the chain, a small amount of ETH will be lost. Because supply growth will halt, this deflationary pressure will theoretically squeeze prices higher.

**Reason for the Halving**

Yes. Bitcoin is an excellent analogy. In this situation, Bitcoin was "Halved," equivalent to "Burning." Both are lowering inflation. The most recent Bitcoin halving occurred on May 11, 2020, when the BTC reward reduced from 12.5 to 6.25. The price of Bitcoin was $8,800 on that day, and it virtually doubled in price during the next six months. And depending on the day of the week and volatility, 1 BTC will cost you almost $30,000 or $60,000 today. Essentially, "halving" generates scarcity, which raises the coin's price. The more precious a coin is, the scarcer it is.

According to analysts, EIP-1559 will reduce sell pressure by around 30%, implying that there would be less ETH available to purchase on marketplaces. According to some observers, the price of ETH might reach $150,000 by 2023. The combination of EIP-1559 and the switch to a proof-of-stake Ethereum 2.0 would be a "triple halving," reducing sell pressure by an estimated 90% Percent — equal to three Bitcoin halvings.

Developers will be working on "The Merger" over the next two years, ending proof of work and ushering in the proof of stake era. The merger might occur by the half of 2022. The change from a mine and dump economy to a stake, and re-stake one will be one of the first visible consequences of this upgrade: Proof-of-stake encourages people to save since the more ETH they have, the more they earn. Proof-of-work promotes sales.

Another significant feature is that the PoS transition will reduce emissions by 90%. As a result, daily block rewards will drop from 12,800 to 1280 ETH, and inflation will drop from 4.3 percent to 0.43 percent, equating to three Bitcoin halvings. Furthermore, EIP 1559 will include fee burning, which will add to the rarity of ETHER and increase its price.

**Ways to Reduce Your Ethereum Gas Fees**

The cost of using Ethereum is continuing to climb, rendering the network unworkable at times. What if you could cut your Ethereum gas costs in half? For its safe functioning, the Ethereum network, like any car, requires gasoline, and it's what we call gas. Decentralized finance (DeFi) transactions are becoming increasingly prevalent as

Ethereum grows in popularity. Unfortunately, due to the high volume of DApps and individual users, the gas charge rises.

## Meaning of Ethereum Gas Fee

When you conduct any transaction on the Ethereum blockchain, you must pay a gas price. The Ethereum blockchain functioning necessitates some computing work, which bitcoin miners provide. Miners are rewarded with ETH (the Ethereum crypto token) to contribute to the Ethereum network's upkeep and security. A block of cryptocurrency transactions is a collection of transactions. Blockchains have different block sizes. Bitcoin's block size, for example, has a theoretical limit of 4MB but averages around 1MB.

Unlike Bitcoin, the block size in Ethereum is determined by the amount of gas spent on every block rather than a data restriction. The current block size restriction is 30 million gas, while the goal size is 15 million gas per block. However, your transaction competes with others for a spot in the next block transmitted to the network for validation. As a result, your rival may pay a priority charge (tip) to enhance the likelihood of their transaction being processed ahead of yours, hence raising the gas fee.

On the Ethereum blockchain, "network congestion" causes "competition" of transactions due to network validation. When more transactions use the Ethereum network for validation, network congestion arises. Because the Ethereum public blockchain has found considerable popularity in decentralized operations like decentralized exchanges (DEX), DeFi, blockchain games, social, ERC-20 token transfers, and marketplaces, transaction volumes are rising. DApps are also offering new features, which makes their functionality more difficult. As a result, a smart contract now has to do more operations. As a result, the already few ETH blocks become crowded as complicated transactions consume more space.

The following suggestions will help you save money on gas while speeding up transaction processing.

**Use Simulation Through DeFi Saver**

You won't know the actual gas fee until you complete the transaction and pay for it. You might, however, simulate your transactions with the DeFi Saver software. You'll start by creating an Ethereum activity recipe, which you'll execute virtually. The real-world simulation will provide you with an expected maximum gas fee in ETH. You may then tweak your entire recipe to save money on gas. To save money on gas, run this recipe on the Ethereum platform.

**Transaction Timing Optimization**

Congestion is the fundamental reason for increasing gas fees. The volume of transactions on Ethereum, on the other hand, changes throughout the day, and you may see a decreased gas fee for a transaction that cost you more ETH just a few hours before. However, determining such timeframes might be time-consuming, and it will also reduce your productivity because you will have to monitor gas fees at different times. As a result, you may go to the Ethereum Gas Charts website to see a detailed graph of gas fees for the week.

Another strategy is to avoid working hours throughout the week. Even if you have to send a transaction throughout the week, do so after midnight.

### Organize Transaction Types

The gas price on the Ethereum blockchain varies depending on the transaction. As a result, you might wish to group similar transactions to save money on gas fees. Consider the case when you have two Ethereum addresses, each with 1,000 tokens. To make greater profits, you intend to lock all of the tokens in a vault of a new DApp. To save money on gas fees, you can send all tokens to one address and then lock 2,000 tokens in one transaction.

### Use DApps Offering Discounts and Reducing Gas Fees

Ethereum projects and DApps provide lower or no gas prices than the market. Balancer is one such platform; It gives a 90 percent gas fee reimbursement in the form of the BAL token. It reduces the gas charge for high-frequency traders by performing deals without leaving the vault. KeeperDAO and Yearn's V2 Vaults are two DeFi programs that combine individual user transactions. Instead of making separate payments, each user pays the gas fee all at once, reducing the gas fee by a significant amount.

### Make use of gas tokens

You may earn ETH as refunds when you erase your storage variables on the Ethereum network. It is the foundation for gas tokens. When gas fees are low, you can produce many gas tokens. Redeem your gas tokens into ETH when you need to complete a network transaction. Use your ETH rewards to pay for the gas. GasToken.io is a well-known startup that allows you to create your gas tokens.

## Assess Network Congestion to Plan Ahead

When there are a lot transactions in the pipeline, your work may be waiting. The gas charge you agreed on has already risen during this wait time. Because you set a gas limit below the current rate, it will fail when miners try to execute your transaction. What's more concerning is that you'll be charged a gas fee for an uncompleted transaction. As a result, planning is essential to save money on gas and avoid penalties. Schedule your Ethereum transactions at off-peak times.

Keep a watch on the Gas Price by Time of Day chart on Ethereum Gas Charts for the current pricing of gas costs according to the local timezone for time-sensitive transactions. To prevent extra fines, carefully estimate the gas charge and select the correct gas limit.

## Accurately calculate Ethereum gas fees

Because it does not account for real-time transaction congestion, your Ethereum wallet may not provide accurate estimates of gas fees. For time-sensitive transactions, you might wish to use specialist tools like Etherscan's Gas Tracker or Gas Now.

These tools examine pending Ethererum transactions on the mainnet. They then provide many estimations for time-sensitive gas fees. You don't pay more than you should or face fines for failing to establish proper gas restrictions.

## Explore Ethereum Layer 2

Due to congestion, transactions on the Ethereum Mainnet (layer-one) are costly. Layer-two solutions are available to assist users in scaling up transactions. Layer-two uses technologies like Rollups and moving transactions to sidechains on this network. As a result, this new procedure saves money on gas and speeds up transaction completion. Layer-two scaling methods like Optimism, Arbitrum, and Polygon are worth looking at.

### Use Crypto Wallets with Optimized or Zero Fees

Using zero-fee crypto wallets is another way to save money on transactions.

### FTX

FTX is a well-known cryptocurrency exchange, trading, and portfolio management tool. You can trade cryptocurrencies for free, and it also does not impose any deposit fees. Furthermore, when you bet the FTT token, you get free withdrawals.

### Dapper ETH

Through Dapper Pass for CryptoKitties, this crypto wallet grants you access to gas-free transactions. To save money on gas, you might wish to buy Dapper Transaction Passes for other DApps. Dapper Transaction Passes are accepted by DApps such as Cheeze Wizards, Decentraland, HyperSnakes, etc. Dapper Passes and Transaction Passes together might save you more money on gas than regular users.

### Digifox

Though gas costs are unavoidable, you may join a queue for a free Pro account on this wallet. In addition, the platform is developing Ethereum layer-two solutions to provide zero-net trading and payment services.

**The burning of \$6 Billion in ETH as Ethereum 2.0 Edges Closer**

Ethereum, the second-largest cryptocurrency, has officially spent almost 2 million ETH using a burn mechanism implemented in 2021. The burning mechanism on Ethereum is hotter than ever, with the crypto's second-largest network destroying nearly 2 million ETH since it was launched in August 2020. Since its debut, the network has burned 2,000,996 Ethereum, according to Watch the Burn, a dashboard that monitors the burn process. In dollars, that amounts to \$5.82 billion permanently removed from circulation.

The burn mechanism, codenamed EIP-1559, was one of many network improvements incorporated in the London hard fork. The Ethereum Improvement Proposal altered the Ethereum network's cost structure. EIP-1559 divides all fees paid to miners for specific Ethereum activity into a basic fee and tips (the latter would go to miners).

The base fee is burnt, which means the coin is destroyed and taken out of circulation. This burn mechanism has fed the "ultra-sound money" meme. According to the meme, when there is a surge in Ethereum activity, the destruction of the circulating supply may outstrip the quantity supplied via block rewards. As a result, there are fewer Ethereum on the market to buy, creating a deflationary impact.

Joe Lubin, Ethereum co-founder and CEO of ConsenSys (which finances an editorially independent Decrypt), cautioned attendees at this year's Camp Ethereal during a fireside discussion that yet another update will put this specific meme into even greater emphasis.

## Purpose of the Burning

The second most popular cryptocurrency network, Ethereum, is purposefully destroying a portion of its supply. Since August 2021, it has limited the supply of its cryptocurrency, Ether, by 65 percent. According to Watch the Burn, an Ether statistics dashboard, it's the equivalent of more than $5.8 billion burned, destroyed, and removed out of circulation. The decrease in available cash is part of a complicated strategy to enhance the blockchain while decreasing the amount of money that crypto miners may earn from each transaction.

## Preventing Gaming of the System

The network deployed Ethereum Improvement Proposal (EIP) 1559 in 2021,. As a result, it splits transaction costs between a basic charge and a tip to the miner, which were previously paid entirely to miners. The miner gets a tip, but the base fee is either burnt or destroyed. Under EIP 1559, the burn is necessary to prevent miners from "gaming the system" with spam transactions, according to Ethereum developer Tim Beiko.

"They could flood blocks with spam transactions if we didn't burn a portion of the transaction fees, raising the minimum charge for everyone but themselves." This, according to Beiko, can also help the network's transaction costs remain stable. Depending on how busy the network is, such fees might add hundreds of dollars to the cost of executing Ether transactions.

According to Beiko, the burn also ensures that transaction fees are paid in Ether, solidifying Ether's status as the Ethereum network's currency. Miners can charge their clients in other currencies or be paid in other currencies, but on Ethereum, they must pay the transaction fee in Ether. Burning Ether's currency can make it deflationary in the long term, reducing its supply and raising its value. However, deflation isn't the aim, and the burn doesn't ensure it, according to Beiko.

While Ether has already lost a significant portion of its value, the networks merge,' a much-anticipated major update to Ethereum that will change the blockchain from proof of work to proof of stake, may lose considerably more.

## The Techniques

Most cryptocurrencies use one of two main consensus techniques. The older two are the proof of work used by Ethereum 1.0, Bitcoin, and many other cryptocurrencies. In contrast, proof of stake, which is used by Ethereum 2.0, Cardano, Tezos, and other cryptocurrencies, is the newer. The energy usage of the two consensus techniques is a substantial difference. Because miners do not need to expend power on repetitive operations while vying to solve the same challenge, proof of stake allows networks to function with substantially lower resource utilization.

The blockchain merged on the Kiln testnet before Ethereum's final conversion to a proof of stake network, with network validators creating post-merge blocks containing transactions. Following the Merge,' the quantity of ETH produced is likely to reduce by 90%, resulting in equivalent fees diminishing Ether's supply by up to 5% every year, according to blockchain analytics firm IntoTheBlock's newsletter.

**Key Takeaways**

- Crypto-friendly Switzerland has made the most progress in giving institutional staking. Digital asset bank Sygnum is now enabling Ethereum 2.0 staking.

- Sygnum's Ethereum staking service will include locking up multiples of 32 ETH for an unspecified amount of time until Ethereum 2.0 is implemented.

- Triple halving is a new protocol that shifts consensus away from intensive proof-of-work and toward proof-of-stake in Ethereum blockchain coins.

- Gas fees are the reward paid to miners for executing transactions on the Ethereum blockchain.

- The Ethereum Improvement Proposal (EIP), one of the numerous network improvements implemented in the London hard fork and the technical name for the burn mechanism, changed the cost structure of the Ethereum network.

# CHAPTER 6

## ETHEREUM 2.0 STAKING

The Ethereum network is increasingly overcrowded, causing transaction costs to increase, making many use cases prohibitively expensive. This is partly due to DeFi programs' success, where users are ready to pay high transaction fees since the transactions are so valuable. Because transaction fees finance existing apps running on the Ethereum blockchain rather than simply transactions, they are referred to as "gas" fees in Ethereum. Due to high gas fees, non-financial DApps (decentralized apps built on top of Ethereum) find it challenging to run on Ethereum.

The Ethereum Foundation has been working on Ethereum 2.0 (Eth2), a network update that improves the Ethereum network's security, speed, efficiency, and scalability. The safety and scalability of the Ethereum network allow it to process more transactions, eliminate bottlenecks, and accommodate more use cases, especially outside of finance.

A staking mechanism will replace Ethereum's current mining procedure as part of this update. Staking is the process of actively engaging in transaction validation on a proof-of-stake (PoS) blockchain (similar to mining). Anyone with the minimum requisite coin balance can validate transactions and receive staking rewards on these blockchains. You can trade Ethereum on sites like Coinbase, Binance, and Kraken. In the context of financial transactions,

Ethereum presently handles 15 transactions per second, which is rather sluggish. On the other hand, Proof-of-stake allows the Ethereum blockchain to execute 100,000 transactions per second, greatly extending the range of projects and applications you can create on it.

This chapter will walk you through ETH staking, including how to stake Ethereum, how Ethereum staking works, and the incentives for ETH 2.0 staking.

**Staking Model**

Staking is a method used by PoS blockchains to safeguard the chain and create new blocks; it is the process of choosing validators to create a new block. The chance of a validator being selected to develop/validate a block is proportional to the number of coins. As a result, anyone with a small number of coins may participate in staking and earn extra coins in proportion to the quantity they stake.

Individuals must stake their Ether (ETH), the Ethereum blockchain's native coin, to become validators on the network. Like miners in proof-of-work, Validators are in charge of organizing transactions and constructing new blocks so that all nodes can agree on the network's state. Validators are in charge of processing transactions, storing data, and adding blocks to Ethereum's new consensus architecture, the Beacon Chain. Validators get interest in their staked coins, denominated in Ether, as a reward for their active involvement in the network.

Users must deposit 32 ETH to become a validator on Ethereum. Validators are in charge of producing blocks at random and double-checking and verifying any blocks they do not create. Positive validator behavior gets rewarded with the user's stake For example, if a user goes offline (fails to validate), they may lose a portion of their share or lose their entire investment if they engage in willful collusion. Depending on the PoS system, users may also be able to delegate their stake to another user who can act as a validator on their behalf.

This type of Staking gives participants a passive income stream while also assisting in the security of Ethereum 2.0, the Ethereum network's future iteration.

**Ethereum Staking Mechanism**

Unlike proof-of-work or PoW-based blockchains, the PoS-powered blockchain bundles 32 blocks of transactions during each round of validation, which takes an average of 6.4 minutes. These sets of blocks are referred to as "epochs." When the blockchain adds two more epochs, it is regarded as irreversible, meaning that you can consider an epoch complete.

The Beacon Chain separates stakers into 128 "committees" and allocates them to a shard block at random. The system gives each committee a slot and time to propose a new block and verify the internal transactions. Each epoch contains 32 slots, which means 32 committees must complete the validation procedure. After assigning a committee to a block, the system grants a member the exclusive authority to propose a new block of transactions at random. The remaining 127 members, on the other hand, vote on the proposal and attest to the transactions.

The Beacon Chain takes status data from shards and sends it to nearby shards to maintain the network in sync. The Beacon Chain will be in charge of the validators, from registering their stake contributions to distributing rewards and punishments. The practice of sharding divides the Ethereum network into many sections known as shards.' Each shard would have its state with its own set of account balances and smart contracts.

Once a majority of the committee has certified it, the new block is put on the blockchain, and the system constructs a "cross-link" to confirm its insertion. Only then does the staker chosen to propose the new block receive their reward.

During the cross-linking process, the system reconciles individual shard states with the main chain, i.e. the Beacon Chain. The final form of each shard must reflect on the Beacon Chain through cross-linking. A transaction is complete when you cannot modify part of a block in a distributed network. To do this in proof-of-stake, Casper, a complete protocol, gets validators to agree on the state of a block at specific checkpoints. If two-thirds of the validators agree, the block is completed. Validators will lose their entire investment if they try to reverse this later with a 51% attack.

**Ethereum Staking Rewards**

In ETH 2.0, you calculate rewards using annualized interest rates and an inverse square root algorithm. In layman's terms, the smaller the total quantity of ETH pledged, the lower the validator incentives. Block proposers and attesters have different payment structures. The block proposer receives ⅛ of the base reward, known as "B," while the attester gets the remaining ⅞ B, adjusted based on how long it takes the block proposer to submit their attestation.

The attester must submit it as soon as possible to obtain the whole ⅞ B award. Each slot that passes without the attester, including the attestation to the block, reduces the reward. If two slots pass before the attestation, the award is decreased by 7/16 B, 7/32 B if three slots pass, etc.

The primary reward has a significant influence on the issuance rate of Ethereum 2.0. The bigger the number of validators linked to Ethereum 2.0, the lower the base reward per validator. This is because the base payment is inversely proportional to the square root of the total balance of all Eth 2.0 validators.

## Risks of Staking Ethereum

If you're serious about staking Ethereum, make sure you have all of your bases covered and consult a financial counsellor. Although the benefits appear to be great, there are hazards associated.

## Worth of Ethereum 2.0

While this may not be an issue in the long run if Ethereum 2.0 is exceptionally high, keep in mind that the value of Eth 2.0 is unknown and will most certainly differ from Ether. If you believe Ethereum 2.0 will be a successful project, you should consider running a validator node.

## Liquidation

Another key concern is a lack of liquidation. Earned and staked ETH cannot be withdrawn until Ethereum 2.0 is implemented, which might take up to two years or more. If you are not a long-term holder and intend to sell Ethereum during this or the next bull run, this may not sit well with you. Running a validator node might be a good option if you feel cryptocurrencies are the way of the future and want to hold on to them for a long time. You have significant incentives to keep ethereum for five years or more with the benefits you will get. Although it is possible to stake Ether on exchanges to increase liquidity, this does not directly benefit the network or decentralization.

## Bugs

Even though Ethereum is one of the most dependable blockchain networks available, powering hundreds of apps utilized regularly, you should be aware of any vulnerabilities. In the event of a severe problem, you may lose part or, in the unlikely worst-case situation, all of your Ethereum. Although there have been few cases of this occurring, be aware that it is possible.

That said, there are already a lot of investors operating validator nodes, so you're not completely alone. You'll be joining a large Ethereum community that has long supported and invested in the blockchain.

## How to Stake Ethereum

You can do Ethereum staking in a variety of ways. Custodial staking solutions take care of the entire staking procedure for you. They will set up the node for you when you deposit Ether. They also take care of running and managing the node, so you don't have to.

The primary difference between solo and other staking systems is that you do not have control over the private key of the validator node. Your assets are managed and controlled by the staking provider. In exchange for their services, they take a percentage of your rewards.

Setting up a staking node on the new Ethereum network requires clients with Ethereum 1.0 and Ethereum 2.0, and Ethereum clients are just programs that let nodes connect with the Ethereum network.

Users will need a computer with sufficient memory capacity to download the old and new Ethereum blockchains. Ethereum 1.0 contains over 900 terabytes of data and expands at roughly 1 gigabyte each day. Validators must also ensure that they always link their nodes to the blockchain. As a result, having a strong internet connection is essential. You must transfer at least 32 ETH to the Ethereum staking contract address after installing the validator program on your PC.

You'll need to create two keys: signing and verifying transaction blocks and another for cash withdrawal. You won't be able to make your withdrawal key until Eth1.0 and Eth2.0 combine in 2022. Before transferring money to the staking contract address, you must first travel to the ETH 2.0 launchpad and fulfill the instructions. This payment confirms your status as a validator, and it also gives the network a way to penalize rogue validators that intentionally or inadvertently compromise the Ethereum blockchain's integrity. When the blockchain uncovers validator behavior anomalies, the perpetrators' money staked is "slashed." Slashing occurs when an Ethereum 2.0 validator purposefully violates network rules and is removed. A percentage of their staked ETH is taken away as a punishment, and in other cases, the total staked value of 32 ETH is taken away. They get punished for encouraging offline validator nodes to stay connected to the network. The procedure delivers penalties and rewards every six and a half minutes, or epoch.

## Hardware and Software Requirements

When Ethereum 2.0 is released, many individuals will be interested in staking ETH, and users must first ensure that they have the necessary hardware before proceeding. There's a long way to go before real staking can commence. After deciding to participate in Ethereum 2.0 staking, the first step is to learn how to run the validator node. Users who are hesitant to trust a third-party supplier, in particular, will have some work to do. You must connect a validator node to the network at all times, and it appears that employing smaller devices such as Raspberry Pi would not suffice.

Instead, Ethereum 2.0's current hardware requirements are relatively high, and new hardware is required to make a dent. Users must also ensure that their gadgets can stay connected, even if there is a power outage. It will be challenging to overcome all of these obstacles.

The following are the current hardware recommendations:

- Operating Systems: Linux 64-bit, Mac OS X, and Windows
- Intel Core i7-4770 or AMD FX-8310 processor (or better)
- RAM: 8 gigabytes
- Storage: 100GB SSD space available

Furthermore, broadband internet is required, although these validator nodes can operate on mobile data connections if necessary. Computer hardware from a previous generation can also accomplish the job, but it may take more monitoring and maintenance to keep it running well.

**Finding the Right Software Client**

Being an Ethereum 2.0 validator entails more than just figuring out the hardware; and it's just as essential to pick the correct software supplier for the job. Several Eth2 clients are currently available, but they all offer something unique. Over time, more software clients may become accessible, and for the time being, these four will suffice.

Prysm and Lighthouse, two of the four Ethereum 2.0 clients available, may appeal to most consumers. Teku is primarily built for institutional needs, although Nimbus can function on mobile hardware. This latter client will be of importance, as smartphones and tablets are now considered mini computers.

To keep in mind, users must also operate an Eth1 node. They will be unable to access Ethereum 2.0 and its staking element without this node, and the node will keep an eye out for deposits of more than 32 ETH. OpenEthereum, Geth, Besu, and Nethermind are among the clients available for an Eth1 node. Being an Ethereum 2.0 validator may appear intimidating with all of these standards, and it's understandable, given the number of different options to tick. It remains to be seen if this effort will be beneficial after all is said and done. Nobody knows how effectively Ethereum's Staking will work or its effect on the ETH price.

**Best Platforms to Stake for Ethereum 2.0**

With ETH staking services becoming more competitive, let's watch which platforms are the best in terms of simplicity of use, security, and predicted profits. We'll briefly describe each of our recommended

ETH staking platforms and some of its benefits and drawbacks in this section.

**Coinbase**

Coinbase is a cryptocurrency exchange established in the United States and noted for being regulatory compliant and institution-friendly. The exchange went public in April 2021, and its shares are traded on the Nasdaq stock exchange. Staking ETH on Coinbase is simple, but there are specific prerequisites to meet before getting started. This requires residing in an eligible nation and having your ID documents verified, and Staking is limited to individual accounts (no business accounts).

There is no minimum amount of ETH a user must stake, although Coinbase does have a changeable maximum limit to "control network restrictions." Staking benefits are given daily and may be recorded in a user's "lifetime rewards" balance, although they can't be accessible until Ethereum 2.0 launch. Staking costs on Coinbase are among the highest in the market, with a 25% commission taken out of all staking payouts.

There are no minimum staking limits and a configurable maximum to control network restrictions. Payments are made daily into a "lifetime rewards" account that you cannot access, and the staking balance is not affected. They have an interest rate of up to 6%. Simply go to their asset page and follow the instructions. You can do all these on a mobile device. Staking fees on Coinbase are astronomical, with a whopping 25% commission on all returns obtained.

## Pros of Coinbase

- Trustworthy platform
- Institutional grade
- There is no ETH minimum requirement.

## Cons of Coinbase

- ETH and rewards that have been staked are useless until Ethereum 2.0 is released.
- The costs of 25% are pretty hefty.

## Kraken

Kraken is a well-known American cryptocurrency exchange that has been functioning since 2013. The exchange allows users to stake any amount of ETH using a simple user interface that includes additional buttons for quickly selecting 25%, 50%, 75%, or 100% of their ETH value.

Although ETH cannot be unstaked, Kraken provides stakers with "ETH2.S" tokens that reflect their staked currencies, giving them some flexibility. You can trade these on an ETH-ETH2.S market open to all nations except the United States and Canada. Staking rewards will be paid in ETH2 (not ETH2.S), which cannot be deposited, withdrawn, or exchanged. Stakers are charged a 15% fee on all Kraken's rewards, which are reflected in their advertised RPY rate.

## Pros of Kraken

- Long-standing exchange
- Staking UI that is simple

- Marketable ETH2.S tokens represent a stake.

**Cons of Kraken**

- High commission rates (15 percent)
- The US and Canada do not have access to the ETH2.S marketplaces.

**Binance (Non-US)**

Binance is the world's biggest cryptocurrency exchange, with significant daily trading volumes and many cryptocurrency-related services. Staking ETH on Binance requires only one click and rewards the user with an equivalent number of BETH tokens. On-chain rewards are distributed as BETH directly into a user's spot account, and these tokens represent their stake in the pool.

You can use BETH tokens for other purposes on the Binance platform, but only while they are in your spot wallet will they receive staking interest. While you cannot withdraw staked ETH, you can readily convert BETH to ETH one-to-one. Binance has promised to provide customers 100 percent of all on-chain incentives, meaning they will not take any commission. The amount of ETH you can stake has almost no minimum or maximum constraints.

**Binance Pros**

- One-click Staking
- Stakeholders get BETH, which they can use while their staked ETH is unavailable.
- There are no minimum or maximum restrictions.

- There are no commissions, and users earn 100% of the incentives.

## Cons of Binance

- If users move their BETH out of their spot wallet, they will not receive interest.

- Some users may get inconvenienced by Binance's lack of support for fiat currency trading.

## StakeWise

StakeWise is an Ethereum 2.0 staking platform that supports custodial and non-custodial staking. Since May 2020, a beta version of the platform has been in use, allowing it to be thoroughly examined. The platform's core offering, StakeWise pool, is custodial and serves modest stakers. Users can pool as little as one eth using a user-friendly dashboard to generate real-time revenues.

Stakers get a certain number of sETH2 tokens to reflect their stake in the pool and rETH2 token payouts, and ETH2 tokens must be owned (in rETH2). All staker rewards received through this method are subject to a 10% commission fee. StakeWise also offers a "StakeWise Solo" option, allowing users with the needed 32 ETH to stake their node. For a monthly cost of 10 DAI, this is a non-custodial alternative that uses StakeWise's infrastructure to run the validator.

## Pros of StakeWise

- No minimum limit
- Easy-to-use dashboard
- Issues tokens that reflect pool stakes and payouts.

- Competitive 10% charge
- Solo validators have a non-custodial option

## Cons of StakeWise

- Other centralized platforms and exchanges have a more established reputation
- Staking options for non-custodial Ethereum

## Rocket Pool

Rocket Pool is a decentralized ETH 2.0 staking mechanism backed by ConsenSys and other well-known blockchain companies. The protocol was first created in late 2016 utilizing Vitalik's mauve paper, and it has been in development since 2017. Anyone with more than 0.01 ETH can join the Rocket Pool platform, which provides stakers with rETH tokens that can be utilized in the DeFi ecosystem when their ETH is unavailable.

Commission rates fluctuate depending on supply and demand, and it's unclear what range this may apply to. Users may also receive a more significant return (with no fees) by staking 16 ETH for their node, half the typical node requirement. Small stakers account for the remaining 16 ETH. Any losses caused by defective nodes are shared across the entire platform, reducing risks for individual users.

## Pros of Rocket Pool

- Backed by ConsenSys
- rETH tokens are distributed to stakers.

- Trading rETH for ETH + incentives allows for an early departure.
- A validator node costs only 16 ETH (and there are no fees!).
- Risk is shared.

**Cons of Rocket Pool**

- Commissions vary and are not specified directly.
- Gas fees may exceed the benefits for small stakers.

## Blox Staking

Blox Staking is a decentralized Ethereum staking platform for independent nodes/validators only, requiring stakers to hold a minimum of 32 Ethereum. Blox previously obtained funding from the Ethereum Foundation to create Secret Shared Validator (SSV) nodes for Ethereum staking, which provide a safe means to split validator keys among non-trusting operators. Through a desktop program, users may maintain total control over their private keys while avoiding the maintenance and security of their validator node. Early adopters may use Blox Staking for free, but users must pay for their cloud subscription, usually costs $7 to $15 each month.

**Pros of Blox Staking**

- Early adopters get it for free.
- Non-custodial
- The Ethereum Foundation has given its support.

**Cons of Blox Staking**

- Only independent validators (32 ETH minimum)

- Users are responsible for paying for their cloud services.

## Allnodes

Allnodes is a non-custodial platform that allows users to stake their coins across multiple networks, including Ethereum 2.0. It provides hosting plans with differing levels of uptime and capacity. Allnodes only offers independent validator staking for Ethereum 2.0, which needs a minimum of 32 ETH. Staking for ETH 2.0 starts at $5 per month and allows various fiat and cryptocurrency payment options. The platform has an easy-to-use user interface, 24/7 customer service, and additional benefits like bonuses, rewards challenges, airdrops, contests, etc.

## Pros of Allnodes

- Non-custodial
- Simple user interface
- 24 hours a day, 7 days a week Customer service is available
- Extra benefits
- No commission.

## Cons of Allnodes

- Only independent validators (32 ETH minimum)
- There is very little information about the firm on the website.

## Lido

Lido is a decentralized, open-source ETH 2.0 staking platform that allows users to stake any amount of ETH. Since it is governed via a DAO-controlled smart contract, staking providers never have direct access to customer funds. Lido holders get stETH tokens in a 1:1 ratio to their staked ETH. stETH is a token that you can use in the DeFi ecosystem to represent staked ETH and prizes, and you receive staking payouts in stETH in real-time.

All staking payouts are subject to a 10% commission fee distributed between node operators, the Lido DAO, and an insurance fund.

## Pros of Lido

- Decentralized and open-source
- For liquidity, stakers get stETH tokens.
- The network distributes rewards in real-time.
- Fees are reasonable (10 percent)
- Insurance fund.

## Cons of Lido

For small stakers, gas fees are excessive.

## How to Stake on Coinbase

Staking is an essential aspect of Ethereum's shift to proof-of-stake. Let's look at why Ethereum staking is crucial and how staking Ether on Coinbase may help you start collecting interest on your cryptocurrency.

## Step 1: Create a Coinbase account

If you don't already have one, you'll need to establish a Coinbase account using the Coinbase mobile app. Signing up with Coinbase is simple: simply input your name, email address, and location, then select a secure password. After creating an account, you'll need to authenticate your identity for tax purposes. Your driver's license, the last four digits of your Social Security number, and your date of birth are all documents you'll need. You may buy any cryptocurrency supported on Coinbase's exchange once you get authenticated.

### Step 2: Purchase Ethereum tokens

To stake Ethereum, you must first acquire Ether tokens. Coinbase allows you to purchase Ethereum tokens directly, making it simple to purchase and stake your Ethereum tokens in one spot. You may buy Ether tokens using a market order or a limit order, much like stocks. Market orders will buy Ether tokens at market price, and limit orders will buy Ether tokens only if the price reaches a predetermined price you specify when placing a limit order.

### Step 3: Sign up for the waitlist

Unfortunately, you cannot immediately stake Ethereum tokens on Coinbase. Coinbase has developed a queue to place you in line to stake your Ethereum tokens because of the huge demand. The waiting period varies, but the sooner you sign up, the sooner you may start earning interest on your Ethereum tokens. If you wish to begin staking immediately, Kraken provides Ethereum staking with no waiting period.

### Step 4: Stake your Ethereum tokens

Because Coinbase manages the validator nodes, all you need to do is stake any amount of Ether tokens, and the exchange will handle the rest. Once you've staked your Ethereum tokens on the Eth 2.0 network, you can sit back, relax, and watch your cryptocurrency portfolio grow interest without doing anything.

## Pros and Cons of Staking Ethereum

Consider your investment objectives before determining whether or not to stake your Ethereum tokens. Cryptocurrencies are one of the most volatile asset classes. Thus, if you decide to stake Ethereum, you should have a high-risk tolerance. You will receive income on your principal investment by staking Ethereum. This interest is paid in Ether tokens and is expected to settle at roughly 4% to 8% yearly. This is advantageous if you believe Ethereum will gain value since your interest will also rise in value.

The most significant danger of staking your Ether tokens is the volatility of Ethereum. If Ethereum tokens lose value, you won't be able to sell them since Eth 2.0 hasn't yet been released. Only investors that consider Ethereum as a long-term investment should stake it.

## Staking Rewards on Coinbase

The yearly payouts for staking your Ethereum tokens on Coinbase are roughly 7%. This rate changes based on the quantity of Ethereum invested in Eth 2.0. Anticipate interest to decline until Eth 2.0 is released. Validators will earn incentives for transactions on Ethereum's blockchain after Eth 2.0 replaces the present Ethereum network.

Additionally, staking your Ethereum on Coinbase will earn you 25% less interest than staking it yourself. You'll need 32 Ether tokens to stake your crypto as an independent node, which you may buy using Ethereum software wallets like Argent. If you don't have 32 Ethereum tokens to stake but still want to earn interest, you can stake any amount of Ether on Coinbase.

**Key Takeaways**

- A staking mechanism will replace Ethereum's current mining procedure as part of the Ethereum update. Staking is the process of actively engaging in transaction validation on a proof-of-stake (PoS) blockchain (similar to mining).

- Proof-of-stake is a distributed consensus process used by blockchain networks to obtain consensus. Staking is a method used by PoS blockchains to safeguard the chain and create new blocks; it is the process of choosing validators to create a new block.

- Anyone with the minimum requisite coin balance can validate transactions and receive staking rewards on these blockchains. You can trade Ethereum on sites like Coinbase, Binance, and Kraken.

- Users can do Ethereum staking in a variety of ways. Custodial staking solutions take care of the entire staking procedure for you. They will set up the node for you when you deposit Ether, and they also take care of running and managing the node.

- Slashing occurs when an Ethereum 2.0 validator purposefully violates network rules and is removed. A percentage of their staked ETH is taken away as a punishment, and in other cases, the total staked value of 32 ETH is taken away.

# CHAPTER 7

## ETHEREUM 2.0 DEVELOPMENT AND DEFI

### The Need for Ethereum 2.0 in DeFi

Ether is the second-largest cryptocurrency, although it can only execute 15 transactions per second. Furthermore, gas usage and restrictions create a fee market, and consumers must often fight for transactions and smart contracts to be completed swiftly to pay higher gas rates. NEO, for example, can theoretically execute 10,000 transactions per second, implying that Ethereum has a long way to go.

While it is possible to increase the gas consumption limit, which was introduced in September 2019, it comes at a high cost since it expands an already large blockchain. While Bitcoin's chain is larger, just 283 GB have been mounted on it after more than ten years of blockchain history. The Ethereum chain, which is less than seven years old, is now almost as resource-intensive as Bitcoin, and the problems will likely worsen as the DeFi ecosystem grows.

As a result, Ethereum appears to be in serious need of new solutions. While some, such as Plasma and Raiden, are being developed alongside Ethereum 2.0, the official Ethereum 2.0 and other layer-two solutions are not.

## Transition Period

Users who wish to stake Ether in Phase 0 will have to submit their currencies to a one-way smart contract. This means that any Ether left on the existing network during Phase 0 will only be useable on the previous blockchain after the Phase 1.5 "merger," at which point the PoS and chain sharding capabilities will be available to all of Ethereum.

The transfer to Ethereum 2.0 will take time for DeFi and DApps, according to Jack O'Holleran, the CEO of Skale Labs, which built the Skale Network blockchain platform based on Ethereum. Most will likely wait until the merger and transition "at their leisure." In the DeFi market, the transaction time between the present version of Ethereum and Ethereum 2.0 does not appear to be a considerable worry. While this time is unlikely to influence DApps directly, "any uncertainty or technological challenges that arise might hinder activity," so it's worth considering.

## Advantages of Ethereum 2.0 to DeFi

When fully implemented, we expect the PoS mechanism to impact DApps, notably in the DeFi market. The move will boost the entire ecosystem by allowing ETH transactions and DApps to compete with other blockchains. The sharding chains and PoS consensus architecture will tackle some of the essential concerns with DApps.

The sharding functionality in Ethereum 2.0 will allow 64 chains to run in parallel, significantly increasing transaction speed and throughput. Users will be able to spend Ether across several chains since they will be interoperable. The responsibility of maintaining the blockchain history, on the other hand, will be split among numerous chains, allowing the network to be more accessible while yet remaining safe and retaining classic DeFi functionality.

In one way, ETH 2.0 will affect the dynamics of DeFi: we may see reduced congestion with transactions in DeFi, and the staking mechanism may cut transaction fees. According to Vitalik Buterin, the most crucial aspect of sharding is that it does not impair DeFi composability. DApps will be impacted, especially in the long run. As the Ethereum ecosystem grows, more DApps and individuals utilizing them will necessitate more resources. Sharding addresses this issue to some extent. As new solutions emerge, the community may continue to invest time and resources in the DeFi and DApp arena without concern about incurring "technical debt."

While Ethereum 2.0 appears to be promising for the DeFi space, it is not without danger, so developers continue working on Ethereum 1.0 even as Ethereum 2.0 is being rolled out. The benefits of Eth 2.0 significantly outnumber the risks. Unlike Bitcoin, which is unlikely to evolve much, Ethereum must fundamentally adapt if it is to realize its mission and compete with emerging competitors like Cardano, Flow, Near, and others. However, this does not indicate that there aren't any significant risks. It's a long shot, but Eth 2.0 might sabotage the entire enterprise if managed poorly.

**Booming DeFi**

The debut of Ethereum 2.0 produced a lot of price swings. The price peaked at roughly $670 shortly after the introduction but then fell somewhat in line with the rest of the altcoins during the following days. The hype was most noticeable in DeFi, where ETH 2.0 was critical in increasing the total value locked in the projects. According to experts, we expect this trend to continue. The effects are likely to accelerate participation in DeFi markets, as DeFi builders will be able to improve their products by order of magnitude."

Yearn.merger Finance's with decentralized exchange SushiSwap, which was only the latest in a long series of collaborations obtained by Yearn.Finance, has helped to this tremendous development, as have other reasons, such as the current bull run in crypto. In addition, Uniswap's yield farming was liquidated, resulting in a significant increase in TVL on other protocols such as SushiSwap and Bancor.

Despite the considerable increase in TVL, total transaction volume decreased. In November 2020, transaction volume exceeded $41 billion, a decline of 12% from the previous month. This might be explained by people opting to stake their funds on Eth2 rather than moving them. This was one of the requirements for the launch of ETH 2.0 since each of the 16,384 validators was required to stake 32 ETH to indicate the new chain's activation. The November reduction in transaction volume may readily be explained by the 524,288 ETH locked up in the deposit contract.

Aside from the billions, another indicator of DeFi's supremacy in TVL is that DeFi protocols account for 99 percent of Ethereum transaction volume. DeFi's high payouts still draw users who are unlikely to match ETH 2.0 staking rewards. Users are also likely to stay with Ethereum during this transition if promising blockchain-based applications continue to function effectively. Furthermore, the update's enhancements may attract a more cautious institutional audience.

## Drawbacks of Ethereum 2.0 on DeFi

The DeFi market will most certainly profit from Ethereum 2.0's speedier and more scalable network once it is fully operating. Certain industry actors, however, suggest that there may be some disadvantages. The change will impact the DeFi ecosystem to a PoS consensus. Those that keep ETH in their wallets get rewarded with interest. Staking's compensation may be able to compete with yield farming and other DeFi goods because they fundamentally have very similar incentive mechanisms. While this may take some time to manifest, the possibility of considerable rewards in Eth2 might cause a conflict and reduce the motivation to use DeFi. Innovative solutions to this problem, such as tokenized ETH 2.0 bonds, are being explored.

By transferring a token issued by a fully collateralized smart contract to a creditor, validators can get cash in unlocked original Ether. There is a promise to the creditor that when the blockchain merges and the lockup ends, the creditor will immediately recover the initial 32 ETH plus any accumulated staking rewards.

Another significant concern is that the old and new Ethereum blockchains are now active. As stated earlier in the book, we expect the transfer to the new chain in 2022, assuming all developmental milestones are met, but not without significant risks. Although DeFi protocols may migrate smoothly, there remains the danger of minor hiccups or even catastrophic losses.

## Ethereum Bonds

The locked Ether is a contract that offers a series of dependent future cash payments, similar to some forms of bonds. Tokenized ETH 2.0 bonds are what DeFi-ers will build. Validators can receive funds in unlocked original Ether by transferring a token created by a fully collateralized smart contract to a creditor in exchange for a promise that the creditor will automatically receive when the blockchain merges and the lockup ends the original 32 ETH plus the accumulated staking rewards.

These "bonds" would receive a 20% yearly income based on staking reward forecasts incorporated into the system's monetary supply before falling on a sliding scale as the total amount staked rises, the exact date when the cash will become free and the value of Ether in dollar terms at that moment is unknown. Both are contingent on how effectively and quickly Ethereum developers achieve their aim of a fully integrated Ethereum 2.0 transition. They are also contingent on whether the Ethereum community believes the migration to the new proof-of-stake method is worthwhile.

As a result, market pricing for tokenized locked ETH bonds might gauge how well these parts are coming together. It remains to be seen whether this creates a positive feedback loop that provides developers with real-time sentiment signals to help them gauge whether the market believes they are on track to meet their objectives or whether it creates misaligned incentives to rush through upgrades that aren't yet ready.

## DeFi Solutions Becomes More Competitive

Decentralized Finance occupies a significant position in the Ethereum ecosystem, accounting for 60% of the total value of Ethereum DApps as of May 2020. DeFi DApps already hold over 2.5 million Eth (about $600 million), and the amount is projected to rise as users seek alternatives to traditional financial services.

Unlike established competitors, like the Visa network, which can handle hundreds of transactions per second, scalability remains a stumbling issue for decentralized finance applications (tps). The Ethereum network is currently restricted to fewer than 50 tps at most. The Eth 2.0 update enables developers to improve scalability through technical methods such as sharding, which are projected to significantly increase the number of transactions per second on the network. This might make DeFi apps more comparable to standard solutions.

## Effect of Staking on DeFi

Although sharding and PoS have apparent network benefits, the latter will affect how Ether is created. Staking allows anybody with 32 or more ETH to acquire new coins by staking their existing ones, introducing a punishment mechanism for any harmful activities on the network while rewarding those that execute transactions properly.

While there are arguments for and against the PoS approach, it's worth noting that in its most basic form, it's similar to lending — the most popular application for DeFi applications — in that users lock their ETH to collect interest.

## What The Future Hold

There appears to be agreement on Ethereum 2.0's favorable impact. However, as previously said, there may be some disadvantages, from technological hazards to a shift in DeFi and liquidity dynamics. With a successful transition to Ethereum 2.0 posing a danger to DeFi's growth, some predict a bright future for the NFT industry, which has been expanding rapidly throughout 2020 and is not in direct conflict with the staking paradigm that underpins Eth2.

## Key Takeaways

- When fully implemented, we expect the PoS mechanism to impact DApps, notably in the DeFi market. The move is expected to boost the entire ecosystem by allowing ETH transactions and DApps to compete with other blockchains.

- The sharding chains and PoS consensus architecture will tackle some of the essential concerns with DApps.

- The sharding functionality in Ethereum 2.0 will allow 64 chains to run in parallel, significantly increasing transaction speed and throughput. Users will be able to spend Ether across several chains since they will be interoperable

- While Ethereum 2.0 appears to be promising for the DeFi space, it is not without danger, so developers continue working on Ethereum 1.0 even as Ethereum 2.0 is being rolled out

- Although DeFi protocols may migrate smoothly, there remains the danger of minor hiccups or even catastrophic losses

- The locked Ether is a contract that offers a series of dependent future cash payments, similar to some forms of bonds.

# CHAPTER 8

## METAVERSE AND ETHEREUM 2.0

**Metaverse Coin on Ethereum**

Ethereum remains the most popular platform for dApps and Metaverse currencies, and Ethereum's blockchain contains some of Metaverse's most notable participants as the pioneer in smart contracts and DeFi. This chapter examines the top 5 Metaverse coins built on Ethereum's blockchain, from highest to lowest market cap.

**Axie Infinity (AXS)**

Sky Mavis's Vietnamese company created Axie Infinity, an Ethereum-based NFT collecting game. It contains Axies, charming creatures that users may customize with different traits and send into combat to receive prizes. AXS is the Axie Infinity platform's native ERC-20 coin. AXS is the platform's interface, enabling users to purchase, trade, and sell Axies on their NFT marketplace and stake their tokens for rewards.

AXS is currently trading at $105.69 per share, with a 24-hour trading volume of $435 million. Axie Infinity has a total quantity of 270 million coins, with 60.9 million in circulation. The market capitalization of AXS is $6.42 billion at writing. Binance, Huobi Global, Coinbase, FTX, Crypto.com, KuCoin, Kraken, and more exchanges accept AXS.

## Decentraland (MANA)

Decentraland is a 3D Ethereum-based blockchain-based Metaverse that allows users to own land plots and explore the virtual environment. Several activities are accessible, including casinos, concerts, galleries, and more. Decentraland, the longest-running 3D Metaverse project in crypto, has been accessible to the public since February 2020. The Sandbox, which is presently valued at over $6.9 billion ahead of its alpha debut, is the only other project that comes close to Decentraland offers.

Decentraland may be viewed by visiting their official website and connecting using MetaMask. Make sure your wallet is connected to the Ethereum network, then explore! Decentraland's MANA is now trading at $3.51, with a 24-hour trading volume of $1.1 billion. With a circulating supply of 1.83 billion MANA, it has a market worth of $6.3 billion. You can purchase MANA on Binance, Huobi Global, KuCoin, FTX, Kraken, Crypto.com, and other exchanges.

## SAND (Sandbox)

The Sandbox is currently the best-designed Metaverse project available. It's based on the Ethereum blockchain and comes with a downloaded PC client that outperforms other Metaverse coins in terms of visuals and smoothness. While The Sandbox is similar to Decentraland, it is not restricted by the in-browser experience, allowing gamers to experience a whole new level of immersion and engagement.

The Sandbox is a market leader, with its latest Alpha launch allowing gamers to explore their virtual world. The excitement was justified since the game is well-made, resembling a cross between Minecraft and Fortnite.SAND is currently trading at $5.31 per share, with a 24-hour trading volume of $1.9 billion. With a circulating supply of 913 million SAND, it has a market worth of $4.83 billion. You can purchase SAND on several exchanges, including Binance, Huobi Global, KuCoin, FTX, Bithumb, Gate.io, Crypto.com, Uniswap, etc.

## UFO Gaming (UFO)

UFO Gaming is an Ethereum-based decentralized gaming platform that aims to combine traditional games with blockchain technology. UFO Gaming uses the UFO utility token as its Dark Metaverse's native currency. Each planet in the Dark Metaverse will have its collection of games and enable players to purchase territory using NFTs, much like Decentraland and The Sandbox do. UFO Gaming is now trading at $0.00002245, with a daily trading volume of $16 million. UFO tokens have a market valuation of $578 million and are worth 25.7 trillion dollars. UFO is available on Uniswap, Gate.io, MEXC, LBank, 0x Protocol, ShibaSwap, and other exchanges.

## Alien Worlds (TLM)

Alien Worlds has a decentralized Metaverse that is linked to Ethereum, WAX, and the Binance Smart Chain. It has over 200k members and is presently one of the most popular blockchain-based NFT games. Players in Alien Worlds can rent spaceships and send them on missions to explore the Metaverse, and you can find Trillium as players begin their 2055 expedition. TLM encourages people to play the game by providing real-world rewards.

Players can travel to other worlds, each run by a different Decentralized Autonomous Organization (DAOs). These DAOs receive daily Trillium via smart contracts, and players who are members of that planet's DAO can receive a portion of the TLM. TLM is trading at $0.24 at writing, with a 24-hour trading volume of $216 million. It has a market cap of $227 million and a circulating supply of 914 million TLM. You can purchase TLM on various exchanges, including Binance, KuCoin, Gate.io, FTX, Poloniex, Binance TR, MEXC, LBank, etc.

## Best Metaverse Project on Ethereum

The crypto world and the Metaverse are evolving at breakneck speed. It is challenging to forecast the future of digital worlds and which cryptocurrencies will remain at the top of the finest Metaverse projects. However, it is just another fascinating aspect of the current technological revolution. Even with so many unknowns, here is a list of the best Metaverse projects to get you started on your Metaverse journey.

## Decentraland (MANA)

Decentraland is a well-established Metaverse project with much potential, thanks to people willingly buying virtual land plots for millions of dollars. Yes, millions of (real-world) dollars. But, perhaps most importantly, Decentraland can be viewed as a digital blank canvas for pretty much anything imaginable - and unimaginable. It's a little like the real world, but better. You may shop your favorite brands, go to events, play games, meet new people, start new businesses, and even bet in this Metaverse.

Everything has a real-world feel to it, which is why this Metaverse is still one of the best of its kind. Decentraland is based on the Ethereum blockchain and is completely user-owned, allowing users to establish their settings, avatars, markets, digital infrastructures, and apps. MANA is the cryptocurrency that underpins this humming virtual world, and it can be acquired on several popular crypto platforms. Along with the numerous other advantages already mentioned, the platform has recently witnessed a larger integration of eCommerce solutions, making it an essential destination for advertising and marketing. As a result, it's plausible to expect Decentraland to thrive and rank among the best Metaverse projects in 2022.

## Axie Infinity (AXS)

Unless you've been living under a rock, you've undoubtedly heard of Axie Infinity. This blockchain-based game has captured the world with its cute animal-like characters and the opportunities it offers its players, who have found themselves earning significant sums of money while doing what they enjoy: gaming. Many people have made Axie their full-time job. The Ethereum blockchain Metaverse concept is powered by Axie's native coins AXS and SLP. The governance token is Axie Infinity Shards (AXS). AXS holders can vote on the game's future development plans, such as updates and how the treasury balance is used. AXS has long been regarded as one of the top Metaverse cryptocurrencies. Its value increased by 200 percent in 2021 over the previous year. Smooth Love Potion tokens, commonly known as SLP tokens, can be obtained as prizes in combat or adventure mode. SLP tokens, which you can use to produce Axies, are better. As the game's popularity grew, these animals became increasingly expensive

- a trend still going strong in 2022. And, because gamers can cash out their in-game currency in the real world, that's a model that's not going away anytime soon. Axie Infinity is one of the essential Metaverses to follow this year.

**The Sandbox (SAND)**

The Sandbox is an Ethereum blockchain-based virtual environment. This Metaverse, like Decentraland, focuses on original content development and games. The Sandbox, which draws influence from games like Minecraft and Roblox, employs a 3D voxel technique to allow users to use their creativity and construct worlds in any manner they choose. Using the platform's currency, SAND, anybody may create, control, and sell their game experience. This ERC-20 utility token supports all transactions and interactions in the Sandbox ecosystem. Users have generated over 70 million distinct worlds and habitats, resulting in a thriving non-fungible token market (NFTs). The Sandbox allows its users to construct games, assets, and applications on top of their land parcels and host great content-creation experiences. Each LAND is a non-fungible token on the Ethereum network (ERC-721). Yes, there are several opportunities within their Metaverse that you should investigate.

**Gala (GALA)**

Gala is a blockchain gaming platform that combines the benefits of non-fungible tokens with gaming excitement to make a space where users can freely and easily trade in-game products. Gala features a variety of blockchain-based games classified as social games that focus on forming connections between participants. Mirandus, Spider

Tank, Town Star, Fortified, and Echoes of Empire are the games currently accessible. The degree of control and ownership that this blockchain technology grants players are one of its strong qualities. This is mainly accomplished through GALA, the game's native digital token, which is utilized for network governance, prizes, and node operator incentives across the platform. Gala is also used to purchase digital items, like NFTs, through the game's shop and player marketplace. Gala users may design and modify their avatars, like other blockchain-based games.

**Sensorium Galaxy (SENSO)**

Sensorium Galaxy is a digital Metaverse created in partnership with some of the world's most renowned artists, producers, and media companies. This Metaverse, which is currently in beta, comprises several worlds that serve as a hub for a specific set of experiences. PRISM is the most critical world in Sensorium Galaxy, serving as the gateway to music and entertainment. Exclusive VR performances by chart-topping artists such as David Guetta, Steve Aoki, Armin van Buuren, and others will be available here for Metaverse users. Sensorium can offer an unrivaled multisensory experience that extends to its other worlds, including MOTION, which will host mindfulness and self-exploration, encouraging higher levels of knowledge by combining cutting-edge AI and VR technology with top-tier entertainment content in a virtual reality galaxy.

The in-platform currency, SENSO, is a key feature of Sensorium Galaxy, as it uses blockchain technology to power a fair, transparent, and user-owned decentralized economy. You can use this coin for different transactions, including creating new avatars, purchasing event tickets, and creating unique content.

## Metahero (HERO)

The physical and digital worlds are connected via cryptography and 3D scanning technologies. That's how Metahero characterizes its project, and it's simple to understand why it's garnered so much attention. We expect this platform to bring a new notion of ultra-realistic digital clones that users may personalize and utilize in various Metaverse activities. Because of Metahero's 3D modeling relationship with Wolf Digital World (WDW), each 3D avatar has a lifelike body type and a photo-realistic face, resulting in fantastic AAA avatars. Users can also scan their bodies, save the results as an NFT and use it in the Metaverse. As if that weren't enough, you can customize avatars with various talents and abilities from classes like Close Combat Specialist, Spellcaster, Mentalist, Enchanter, Elementalist, Range Combat Specialist, and Assassin.

Players may level up their Recruits and trade or sell the NFT that fuels their accounts. And, in case you're curious about how it all works, one-of-a-kind Meta scanners are used to scan, print, and create new in-game avatars in addition to scanning. Metahero's native token, HERO, has also proven to succeed in virtual world transactions, and both this Metaverse's unique NFTs and currency are projected to touch larger markets shortly.

## Somnium Space (Cube)

Having a 3D experience is no longer sufficient. With so many beautiful platforms to select from, attracting new Metaverse consumers requires a compelling offer. Somnium Space, fortunately, does just that. This 3D blockchain platform is user-friendly and chock-full of mind-blowing experiences and possibilities to play around with the Metaverse. Newcomers may be unimpressed by the visual quality but what sets it apart is how it allows users to ultimately conceive and personalize both their avatars and the environments around them. Somnium advertises itself as "an open, social, and permanent virtual reality platform," which includes not just a location where users may "live" but also entertainment, communication, e-commerce, and other features.

While the previous Metaverse projects have all been built on the Ethereum blockchain, Somnium has chosen a multi-chain strategy incorporating Solana. This opened up new possibilities for the Metaverse, allowing users to create an NFT Gallery, visit VR concerts with a VR avatar while dancing with a full-body tracking kit, and create new NFT-based worlds and experiences for others to enjoy. Another significant distinction is Somnium's CUBE-based Metaverse economy. The in-platform cryptocurrency facilitates transactions and asset transfers, and it has established itself as one of the most reliable coins among Metaverse's present offerings. Users may also be interested in learning more about the so-called WORLD NFTs, which provide access to unique gaming experiences which you can use to develop wearables. In any case, Somnium is in a league of its own, which explains why it has received the backing of crypto heavyweights like Gemini, Microsoft, and Opensea, to mention a few.

**Star Atlas**

Yes, we've discussed cryptocurrency games, and that's OK. But how about we show you one of the first AAA crypto games globally? Yes, Star Atlas has joined the conversation. All the crypto goodness is crammed into this dramatic and fascinating title. A fantastic plot? Check? Setting that is out of this world? Check? Great neighborhood? Yes. What about monetization possibilities? Yes, without a doubt. Star Atlas is, in a sense, the whole package. We'll let the gameplay to you to discover, so let's speak about another fantastic feature: Star Atlas' two Solana-based tokens, ATLAS and POLIS. The first, ATLAS, functions like a standard in-game currency, allowing users to do tasks like engaging in fights and exploring other realms, and accessing the marketplace. This is significant because most of the game's assets are NFTs, with only a few exceptions.

On the other hand, POLIS allows players to participate in what the makers call the game's "political intrigue." But, probably more crucially, gamers are in charge of deciding game decisions and may even outvote the developers. The project has teased several decentralized features that we expect to pique players' interest and propel them to the top of the Metaverse in 2022.

**Bloktopia**

Bloktopia's skyscraper-themed Metaverse project aims to provide a one-of-a-kind platform where users can study, meet new people, do business, and experiment with various activities over a 21-story structure. Because the building will be incomplete at first, this Metaverse will rely heavily on the contribution and ingenuity of each user. While little is known about this upcoming initiative, which will launch in the coming months, there are some fascinating hints, such as a WWE space. Bloktopia also intends to provide new methods of generating content and revenue for individuals who wish to live in the Metaverse. When it is released, users will have access to levels 1-6. The contents are a mystery, so you'll have to wait to find out.

## Cryptovoxels (CVPA)

Cryptovoxels is a Minecraft-inspired Ethereum-based Metaverse. As a result, this Metaverse has an entire universe of digital infrastructures and land blocks that people may continue to develop. On OpenSea, you can trade assets for ETH, but Cryptovoxels has its currency, the Cryptovoxels Parcel (CVPA). These may be obtained via OpenSea and correspond to landing in Cryptovoxel's Origin City. Users of an NFT retain total ownership of each land piece, known as a Voxel. Players can create and sell virtual properties such as posters, signage, and music recordings. As one of the first Metaverse initiatives, Cryptovoxels has managed to develop a remarkable community that has only grown over time, resulting in even more imaginative and exciting NFTs. As a result, Cryptovoxels will be remembered in 2022. (and beyond).

## Key Takeaway

- The cryptocurrency world and the Metaverse are growing at dizzying pace. It is difficult to forecast the future of digital worlds and which cryptocurrencies will remain at the top of the finest Metaverse projects.

# CHAPTER 9

## NFTS AND ETHEREUM 2.0

**Best NFTs Project on Ethereum**

Over the last year, the NFT industry's explosive expansion has prepared the ground for a slew of fascinating new projects to emerge. These projects present a tempting investment opportunity for smart investors who can spot them early in their development cycle. This chapter will explore the greatest new NFT projects this year and the top upcoming NFTs.

**Lucky Block NFTs**

When it comes to new NFT projects, the Platinum Rollers Club collection from Lucky Block is the top pick. The platform's novel crypto-lottery function has helped Lucky Block become one of the greatest cryptocurrencies on the market. The Platinum Rollers Club, a collection of 10,000 NFTs housed on the Binance Smart Chain, was also launched by the development team.

The NFTs themselves show 2D tickets with a front number. These NFTs, on the other hand, are valuable because of the remarkable benefits they provide to owners, including automatic inclusion into daily prize drawings worth an average of $10,000. Furthermore, 25 NFTs from the Platinum Rollers Club collection are designated as 'Rare Editions,' allowing the owner to win double the prize if their number is drawn. Aside from that, everyone who buys a Lucky Block NFT gets put into a one-time prize draw to win a new Lamborghini Aventador worth over $300,000. The potential upside for this collection is exponential, given that you can mint Lucky Block NFTs for only $1,500.

These Lucky Block NFTs go great with Lucky Block's daily prize drawings, which start on May 15th. Users may purchase $5 tickets using the Lucky Block app to participate in these drawings. Users who own LBLOCK, the native token of Lucky Block, will receive a free ticket to each draw.

The prize pool for Lucky Block's drawings has surpassed $2 million, thanks to a transactional fee imposed on LBLOCK transactions. This implies that NFT owners who possess LBLOCK or buy an entrance ticket will have two opportunities to win each day, one through the NFT reward draw and the other through the main jackpot draw.

The Platinum Rollers Club collection was released on March 19th, and you can purchase them on NFT LaunchPad, a rapidly developing marketplace. We expect these NFTs to sell out rapidly because of the 70x gains recorded by LBLOCK after launching on PancakeSwap and the tremendous excitement produced by Lucky Block's Telegram channel, so buyers must act immediately to get one of these precious commodities.

**Silks**

Silks is another new NFT project that is generating a lot of buzzes. Silks is a blockchain-based Metaverse where users may own, trade, and receive rewards from thoroughbred racing horses. This intriguing project is based on actual occurrences. Therefore, all of the 'virtual horses' in the game have a real-life equivalent. When the real-world horse do well in races, Metaverse participants benefit. Silks is a top-NFT project worth considering because it is also home to the greatest NFT Land and NFT horse racing projects.

The Silks project's virtual environment will allow users to purchase plots of land and build stables to keep their horses. These pieces of land are notable in that they are organized as NFTs, which can be monetized and exchanged on the Silks marketplace. Horses are likewise tagged as NFTs, with new pools of horses produced every year to correspond to the real-world trade of 'Yearlings.'

Each in-game horse will have distinct attributes and characteristics from its real-world counterpart's racing record and training background. Silks maintain the authenticity of this data by rewarding miners with $SLK, the Silks platform's governance token, for validating it. Because a decentralized autonomous organization administers the Silks Metaverse (DAO), this currency will play an essential role in voting on platform modifications. Finally, Silks appears to be one of the year's finest future NFT ventures since it will help gamify the horse-racing experience for a brand new clientele. Furthermore, because Silks is a play-to-earn (P2E) platform, intelligent investors may buy prized horses and make passive income using $STT, Silk's transactional currency.

**VeeFriends**

VeeFriends provides a user-friendly approach to getting started investing in NFTs for people who are new to the market. Gary Vaynerchuk (GaryVee), a well-known marketing guru with a large social media following, founded VeeFriends as an NFT project. The collection contains 10,255 NFTs, which you can purchase on the VeeFriends Marketplace for ETH. The NFTs are computer artwork, with each 'character' displaying characteristics that GaryVee admires.

VeeFriends NFT owners can attend VeeCon, a multi-day business event centered on entrepreneurship, creativity, and innovation. Because GaryVee's business events sell out quickly, having a VeeFriends NFT and receiving entry is considered a significant asset.

You can classify Certain VeeFriends NFTs as 'Presents,' which means that owners will get gifts from GaryVee and the team for the next three years. Finally, 300 NFTs from the collection are designated as 'Access' NFTs, granting GaryVee and the team one-on-one access for three years. VeeFriends is one of the finest new NFT ventures this year because of real-world events and the resale element.

**Decentraland**

Decentraland is likely familiar to those who invest in the greatest Metaverse currencies. Decentraland is an online environment built on the Ethereum blockchain where users may design their avatars and buy virtual property plots. Decentraland's world is notable in that it is organized as a decentralized autonomous organization (DAO), which means that its users have total power over governance concerns.

NFTs are used to structure all of Decentraland's core digital assets. This comprises property parcels (LAND), clothing, cosmetics, and other items. The intriguing part is that you can exchange these NFTs using MANA, the world's native token, on the Decentraland Marketplace with over 100,000 users. You may not only use MANA for in-game transactions, but cryptocurrency investors may also purchase it to bet on Decentraland's development.

Finally, Decentraland's universe has limitless potential, with Metaverse users free to do anything they want with their virtual territory. Advertisers are already taking notice of Decentraland's potential since the Metaverse provides opportunities for businesses to erect virtual billboards. Finally, while GAS costs on Ethereum remain expensive, the network's forthcoming transition to Ethereum 2.0 should resolve this issue, thereby boosting Decentraland's growth.

## Meta Triads

Meta Triads is one of the most intriguing forthcoming NFT mints, containing 10,000 digital art pieces and other features. Humans, Hybrids, and Humanoids are evenly represented in the collection, with the remaining unusual NFT labeled as a 'Triad.' Although the NFTs themselves are beautiful digital art that owners may display, investors are more interested in the additional benefits. Meta Triads' team is working on a marketplace where fashion labels may launch virtual collections in the Metaverse. This is viewed as the next stage in the fashion business, and it has the potential to expand significantly in the following year. As the market grows in sales, all Meta Triads owners will own shares in this marketplace and earn $TRIA. The native token of the marketplace, $TRIA, effectively allows NFT owners to produce a passive revenue stream.

Meta Triads has already attracted thousands of followers on social media, with the project's Discord channel approaching 30,000 members. The collection will be released on March 14th, with each NFT costing 0.18 ETH (about $456 at writing). The Meta Triads NFTs will initially be available for purchase through OpenSea, but investors who miss the drop will be able to acquire them on the secondary market.

## Satoshi Runners

Satoshi Runners is a collection of 7,777 cyberpunk-themed NFTs that aims to combine the allure of digital art with the added advantage of investing. The artwork is animated and depicts individuals with distinct personalities and weapons. The development team has already cooperated with renowned NFT entrepreneurs and a select group of Bored Ape Yacht Club members to guarantee that the digital art is as attractive as possible.

On the other hand, the Satoshi Runners team aspires to build a thriving community of like-minded people, with over 20,000 members on the Discord server. The Satoshi Runners collection is supported by a staking and breeding scheme that lets NFT owners earn recurring cash from their investments. Furthermore, the development team intends to release further collections, with current NFT owners receiving first access to exciting new releases. The Satoshi Runners strategy outlines ambitions to acquire virtual land plots on Sandbox and Decentraland, two of the most popular Metaverse projects in the crypto industry. A 3D Satoshi Runners collection is also in the works, which might work with these Metaverse projects. Overall, Satoshi Runners appears to have a bright future, making it one of the most promising new NFT ventures to invest in.

## Axie Infinity

Axie Infinity is another new NFT game to add to the list. Although Axie Infinity launched in 2018, the project has recently gained traction, and we expect it to develop dramatically this year. Axie Infinity is an Ethereum-based virtual world where users may own and produce 'Axies,' in-world animals with distinct personalities.

These animals are constructed as NFTs, just as Decentraland, and may be exchanged with other users on the Axie Infinity Marketplace. Axie Infinity's native token, $AXS, is used for transactions. Speculative investors can also purchase Axie Infinity to obtain exposure to the virtual world's growth. Axie Infinity appeals to many people because of its combination of investing options and virtual games.

Axie Infinity offers a play-to-earn (P2E) aspect, where users may pit their Axies against the Axies of other players to win prizes. The winner receives $SLP, and you can exchange an ERC-20 token on major cryptocurrency platforms. Looking ahead, as more individuals flock to the platform, the possibility for earning possibilities will grow, which is why Axie Infinity is now generating so much interest in the market.

## WeedGang

The eventual legalization of marijuana in Canada and the United States has spawned a slew of new businesses and projects in the market. WeedGang is an example of a marijuana-themed NFT project, with each NFT showing a different cannabis strain. WeedGang's development staff has great expertise in cultivation and breeding, assuring that this collection has a high level of legitimacy. The NFTs, on the other hand, is only one aspect of the WeedGang tactical game.

Users may earn $RAKS, the game's virtual money, by growing various strains. Finally, this opens the door to a thriving ecosystem where users may monetize their in-game exploits and engage in PvP combat with other players.

WeedGang's crew hopes to give access to real-world events and clubs in addition to virtual notions. We expect WeedGang merchandise drops and even access to other exciting NFT launches in the future. As marijuana legalization progresses, this NFT project will likely gain traction and provide a method for certain groups to earn money via their passions and abilities.

## MekaVerse

MekaVerse is another new NFT project to keep an eye on. MekaVerse is a collection of 8,888 'Mekas,' or digital art NFTs. The artwork is inspired by the popular anime series 'Mobile Suit Gundam,' contributing to the drop's appeal. The MekaVerse NFTs, like other NFT collections, has a unique blend of qualities and attributes, guaranteeing that each piece of art has a certain level of rarity.

MekaVerse's community has exploded since its inception in late 2021, with over 267,000 followers on the official Twitter account. MekaVerse NFT owners join a particular 'faction' in addition to owning a one-of-a-kind piece of digital art. As a result, members of that group have access to unique events. The average price for a MekaVerse NFT is roughly $2,700 at writing, with a sales volume of $236,000 in the previous week. Certain Mekas, however, are considered rarer than others, with Meka #6674 recently selling for nearly $18,000! Overall, MekaVerse NFTs provides a fantastic opportunity for investors to join a growing community while also benefiting from potential value rises.

## Mythia Origins

There are 3,000 cyberpunk characters in Mythia Origins. The characters are intended to be used as user profile photographs, and they all convey a sense of status. Aside from the artwork, Mythia Origins has various benefits. The most exciting aspect is that Mythia Origins NFT owners have access to secret Discord servers where they can discuss upcoming NFT projects with high ROI. Mythia Origins employs analysts that investigate the market and conduct the necessary research to uncover potential enterprises. To keep everyone updated, Discord offers real-time notifications and a dedicated podcast. Owners of Mythia Origins also receive access to a robust software bundle. These tools allow you to view the transactions done by NFT 'whales' and find underpriced NFTs. The development team has also included a portfolio tracker function that will enable you to quickly see how your NFT portfolio performs in terms of profit and loss.

## Implication on Ethereum DApps

In terms of speed and transaction costs, Ethereum 2.0 has the potential to make decentralized finance significantly more realistic. ETH 1.0 can only handle roughly 25 transactions per second (TPS), and that's insufficient for a single DeFi protocol, let alone a blockchain network. Vitalik Buterin previously stated that ETH 2.0's capacity might soon rise to 100,000 TPS after successfully executing each step.

However, Kyle Samani, the creator of Multicoin Capital, feels that this may not be enough if decentralized finance becomes more popular. He warned about the obstacles ahead during a Twitter debate, "Could you kindly explain how you manage to keep the global banking system running at 25 TPS? 2,500 TPS, perhaps? Maybe 25,000? For crypto to work worldwide, I believe you'll need at least 1,000,000 TPS." 1,000,000 transactions per second! This suggests that even when ETH 2.0's new blockchain network is launched, the platform will require further enhancements to meet customer demand.

The impact of ETH 2.0 on existing DApps is one of the main concerns surrounding it. Will we find ourselves in a situation similar to Apple's, where newer iPhones no longer support applications created for previous devices? Finally, there's no guarantee that DApps will no longer be interoperable with this blockchain. A greater risk is that bumps in the road when deploying the network may create business interruption, slowing down activities.

Suppose the Ethereum 2.0 rollout is done correctly. In that case, it might spark a new wave of blockchain innovation as developers flee smaller platforms due to high transaction fees and sluggish confirmation times return. There are presently 1,394 active decentralized apps, according to Dapp.com's market report for Q2 2020. 575 of them, or around 41% of the total, are Ethereum-based. This blockchain was one of the few possibilities for developers who wanted to build their applications back in the heady days of 2017, but they're now spoiled for choice.

With enough time, Ethereum may be able to reclaim some of the market shares it has lost over the years. In Q2, Ethereum doubled the number of active decentralized app users, hitting an all-time high of 1.25 million, according to the Dapp report. The need for DeFi applications was a major factor in this.

**Centralized Ethereum Staking Services**

The release of Eth2 is one of the most significant events in Ethereum's history, allowing supporters and enthusiasts to operate validators, stake Ether, receive rewards, and contribute to the future of the world's most popular distributed network. The potential to use idle ETH for staking and producing passive interest-based revenue is enormous, but the main hurdle for future stakers will be deciding how they will engage. For the technically minded, DIY staking is a possibility, but a staking-as-a-service provider will most likely be the best option for the rest of us.

Staking on Eth2 will undoubtedly alter dramatically, but there are now two types of staking services: centralized and decentralized. This section will look at the distinctions between the two to help you decide which is best for you. Centralized Ethereum staking services are Providers who administer the total ETH staking process on the user's behalf and keep 'custody' of the user's private keys. This might apply to both private keys (custodial staking) or just one (private key staking) (semi-custodial staking).

Several centralized staking companies provide services for different cryptocurrencies today (and soon to include ETH upon mainnet release). Crypto exchanges like Binance and Coinbase frequently offer these services. Users only need to deposit or transfer funds into the exchange, and the provider will take care of the rest.

## Benefits of Centralized Staking

- Onboarding is quick and straightforward.

- Excellent for beginners.

- It does not need a complex infrastructure.

- With less than 32 ETH, you can stake.

- Superior liquidity is maintained.

- Staking is relatively simple by exchanges and centralized service providers (especially if they already hold your assets). This comes at the cost of asset custody, which has its own set of hazards, including significant cutting fines, diminished total benefits, and a higher possibility of asset assault.

## Decentralized Staking Services (dStaking Services)

dStaking Services uses a trustless staking mechanism and hence has no control over the assets of its users. In Eth2, this refers to a service that simplifies validator setup and administration while avoiding storing user private validator keys AND withdrawal keys. This is a critical distinction since many services may claim decentralized and non-custodial while keeping user validator keys in their possession. Although they can't withdraw a user's assets without the withdrawal key, holding the validator key in their possession raises concerns if the service is hacked or if they face group cutting penalties.

## Benefits of Decentralized Staking

- Private keys and ETH are entirely under your control.

- It does not need a complex infrastructure.

- Reduces security threats

- Decentralization of networks and industries is encouraged.

**The Benefit of Ethereum 2.0 Validator**

There is compensation for proposing and attesting the next block in the chain as a validator on Ethereum 2.0. Making valid proposals and attestations would earn you ETH rewards. The rewards are determined dynamically based on the network condition at the end of each epoch. The total amount of ETH staked and the average percent online of validators determine network reward issuance rates.

The system determines the individual validator reward rates by the number of validators operated and the validator's percent uptime. Every epoch (384 seconds 6.5 minutes), validators receive rewards minus penalties. As a result, the payment you anticipate getting if you are randomly chosen to be a validator may differ from what you receive. You may get a notion of the sorts of rewards for staking on Ethereum 2.0 by using the Eth 2.0 calculator. Participating as a validator has the added benefit of earning ETH incentives. However, there is a danger of losing money if the ETH staked on the network is slashed.' You can minimize this risk with a bit of caution.

The first way a validator might lose money is if it goes down and fails to execute its tasks properly. This comes with a bit of penalty: the same as the award you may have earned. You will not lose your investment as long as you are currently participating for at least 50% of the time. A validator might also lose money by publishing inconsistent information about the chain, and the validator gets sliced and removed from the system in this circumstance. Depending on other conditions, the amount cut ranges from 1 ETH to the total stake value. Being slashed is simple to prevent, and it should never happen unless a validator acts maliciously.

## Key Takeaways

- Over the last year, the NFT industry's explosive expansion has prepared the ground for a slew of fascinating new projects to emerge.

- In terms of speed and transaction costs, Ethereum 2.0 has the potential to make decentralized finance significantly more realistic.

- The release of Eth2 is one of the most significant events in Ethereum's history, allowing supporters and enthusiasts to operate validators, stake Ether, receive rewards, and contribute to the future of the world's most popular distributed network.

- Centralized Ethereum staking services are Providers who administer the total ETH staking process on the user's behalf and keep 'custody' of the user's private keys.

- dStaking Services uses a trustless staking mechanism and hence has no control over the assets of its users.

- There is compensation for proposing and attesting the next block in the chain as a validator on Ethereum 2.0. Making valid proposals and attestations would earn you ETH rewards.

# CONCLUSION

Ethereum 2.0 (also known as Serenity) is an update to the Ethereum Network that enhances the network's speed, efficiency, and scalability. Ethereum 2.0 is on its way. The years-long update, which is meant to change the Ethereum platform drastically, is nearing completion. After years as the most popular smart contract network, Ethereum is migrating to a less energy-intensive platform, and some analysts believe Ethereum investors can profit. This will propel Ethereum to new heights by allowing for far more transactions and reducing congestion and excessive gas prices on the Ethereum network. Ethereum 2.0 is a massive update representing the conclusion of five years of study and development.

Never before has a network of the scale and worth of Ethereum attempted to migrate all users and assets to a new decentralized platform while maintaining all activities on the current platform active and functioning. The Ethereum 2.0 update, with all its complexities, has taken several years to complete. However, developers believe that its initial rollout is the most difficult (and maybe most crucial) step on the Ethereum 2.0 timeline. Sharding will be used in Ethereum 2.0 to significantly boost network capacity and minimize gas fees, making sending Ethereum tokens and interacting with smart contracts more affordable. There will also be major economic improvements, with Ethereum 2.0 allowing supporters to stake nodes and earn Ethereum as a passive income. Ethereum 2.0 represents the culmination of years of labor by hundreds of developers in many respects.

According to some analysts, the upgrade might help Ethereum thrive after new blockchain projects have eaten into its market share over the last six months. Related cryptocurrencies might experience a price increase as a result of this update. According to the Ethereum website, present ETH holders can participate in the upgrade by staking or testing the upgrades, but your portfolio stays unchanged. Also, now is an excellent time to brush up on your knowledge of Ethereum mining and the entire blockchain technology. "If you are not an investor but are inquisitive, now is a terrific time to learn." If you are an investor who still does not comprehend, now is a fantastic time to educate and learn. The update will very certainly result in a drop in fresh ETH supply, and demand in the Ethereum blockchain may rise due to the quantity of ETH available to stake.

Dear Reader,

As independent authors it's often difficult to gather reviews compared with much bigger publishers.

Therefore, please leave a review on the platform where you bought this book.

Many thanks,
Author Team

Want Free New Book Launches?
Email us at:
mindsetmastership@gmail.com